# MIXED RACE BRITAIN

## BRITAIN

Julie Jones

Published by

**MELROSE**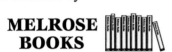
**BOOKS**

An Imprint of Melrose Press Limited
St Thomas Place, Ely
Cambridgeshire
CB7 4GG, UK
www.melrosebooks.com


**FIRST EDITION**


Copyright © Julie Jones 2011

The Author asserts her moral right to
be identified as the author of this work


Cover designed by Matt Stephens


**ISBN 978-1-907732-40-9**

Printed and bound in Great Britain by:
CPI Group (UK) Ltd, Croydon, CR0 4YY

FSC
www.fsc.org
MIX
Paper from
responsible sources
FSC® C013604

# Contents

# Prologue

The contents of this book originally appeared in "Julie Jones' eye on mixed race Britain" in *The Big Eye*, Britain's fastest-growing black newspaper. You can read future columns every month in *The Big Eye*.

# About the Author

Julie Jones was born in the valleys of South Wales in 1957 into a well-known and respected family of costers (fruit merchants) and grew up in a predominantly white environment, to a loving mother who was deaf and a coster father who was killed by a drunk driver.

Julie started her adult life working in a factory making underwear for Marks & Spencer. While working there she was approached by the personnel to enter the Miss Wales contest. Then, too shy, she refused. Although she grew up in a close-knit family, she felt there was something missing from her life. She packed her bags and her life experiences began. She spent many years living in London and Kingston, Jamaica, which have become the basis to her writing.

She worked as a model and now lives in Wales with her two children – one at university – and a stray cat she adopted despite having a cat phobia.

Even to this day, she has dreams to move on, always believing in following her dreams and that it is never too late.

Julie now writes columns for *The Big Eye* newspaper on issues regarding mixed race Britain. *The Big Eye* is the fasting-growing black newspaper in Britain.

# Acknowledgements

I would like to thank my children, Jilly and James, and my sister Jill Richards for supporting and believing in me. Her belief gave me the strength and courage to continue.

I would like to thank my two young cousins, Jonathan and Adam O'Neill, for supporting and believing in me.

I would like to thank my nephew Nicholas Lyons for helping me finish this book, as without his help this book would have lain dormant.

I dedicate this book to the memory of my mother. Thank you, God bless.

This is a book of true experiences and facts on mixed race Britain today.

I write about what I experience and what I know. However, the names of some of the individuals featuring in this book have not been disclosed to protect their identities.

# Columns

## Julie Jones on Race Relations

Hi, I'm Julie Jones from the valleys of South Wales. I have raised two children of mixed ethnic origin in a predominantly white society as a single parent.

As a young girl growing up in this environment I felt something was missing from my life. I wanted to learn about other cultures, especially the Afro-Caribbean culture. It was rare in the 70s for a white girl from the valleys to feel passionate about other cultures, as they were not home to many people of other ethnic origins.

Growing up, I would use my pocket money to buy Reggae and soul music. I even sent away for a box of records directly from Jamaica, which I still have today.

For me, Reggae music is the only music that moves my Erector Pili muscle, which is the muscle which makes the hair all over your body stand up when you feel a strong vibe!

Anyway, enough said about me.

My children have been raised to be confident and proud, and although my daughter respects both cultures, she identifies herself as a young black woman of today.

Her confidence has come from my experiences of living in Kingston, Jamaica. Having spent most of my adult life living and experiencing the West Indian culture, I have passed this passion for living the West Indian lifestyle onto my children, especially the food, which I cook very well indeed!

I remember my Jamaican ex-boyfriend who once said to me:

"There is only one other woman who can cook 'Curry Goat' like this, and that's my mother!" I was very proud of this compliment.

Jamaican people taught me many qualities in life: to be proud, to cook, and also not to let people take liberties with me. This is another important value I pass onto my children.

I was very saddened by one incident of a little girl of mixed origin trying to scrub herself with bleach. Her mother asked me to help; I kept telling the girl how beautiful she was and advised her mother to do the same, and that whatever people said about her, they were jealous because she had the best of both worlds (both cultures).

I invited her mother to bring the child to my home to meet my children and experience a taste of the culture she had missed out on all these years. Ever since that day her mother has not had the worry of her daughter trying to bleach her skin. She has now become proud and interested in her ethnic background.

This is why I strongly believe that the parents of mixed race children should have the opportunity to experience and embrace both cultures. They can then pass this knowledge onto their children, who can become happy in their heritage and confident in their culture.

If my story can be an inspiration to even one of our readers then I feel that I have helped in a big way.

Be strong, be confident and be proud of your heritage.

Peace and God bless,

*JJ*


## Slavery

It's been four hundred years since slavery was abolished. President Barack Obama's wife, Michelle, has ancestors who were slaves, and he once quoted that "she has the blood of slaves running through her veins". How poignant, then, that the most powerful woman in the world came from a background of slavery.

It's hard to believe that a human being could treat another human as a slave, but sadly it was all too true. It must be so distressing for anyone alive today with slaves as ancestors to imagine the life their relations had to endure before them. A life of sheer pain and horror, the humiliation of being made to serve another person that society deemed better than them.

It's hard for me to refer to them as slaves, as the term is so derogatory, but in essence this is how they were treated so the term has to be used to reflect the true indignities they endured. If only they could see now how things have radically changed for the better. They would be so proud, but at the same time, would never have dreamt in a million years they would one day be treated as equals, never mind the four hundred that it did take. The sheer suggestion that a black man would become President of the most powerful nation on Earth would be scoffed at, labelled as ludicrous, but it did happen, and it's for the better. Nor would they have imagined that another black man, Nelson Mandela, would become President of South Africa, an equally unthinkable scenario back in those dark days.

In 1865, slaves were freed after the American civil war ended, it was then that slavery was finally abolished. History is history, we take the bad with the good as it all tells the story of life, so slavery should never be forgotten. It is worth remembering the atrocities of civilisation so they never again happen to a society more learned by the ills of its past. This is why I believe it should be taught in schools, it happened, it was real and we need the youngsters of today to see how privileged they are to live in a world where we've learnt from the evils of times gone by.

It was because of segregation and racism that Dr Martin Luther King voiced his incredibly moving and powerful speech 'I Have A Dream'. I often think how wonderful it would have been if Dr King was alive to see Obama become the United States President, but

I take solace that at least members of his family have done so. There's no doubt in my mind that Dr King contributed to Obama becoming president, it was revolutionary thinking like his that inspired black men all over America and the world.

During the era of slavery, there were quite a few secret relationships going on between masters and slaves which resulted in mixed race children. They called these children 'Molatas'. The first time I heard this term I was on holiday with my children in the Canary Islands some years ago. Someone said to me in conversation that my children were molatas, not being familiar with the term, I asked him what he meant, to which he replied, 'it's a term for mixed race children', it had made its way into the popular vernacular.

One of the true horror aspects of persecution of black people has to be the Klu Klux Klan, imagine being targeted by a vicious group of white supremacists who were intent on harming and even killing you purely because of the colour of your skin. It's frightening to imagine being around at the time, where even a walk down the street could result in being lynched by men grasped and driven by evil.

It's known that when the slave trade was abolished, the slaves were then offered a percentage of land so they could earn a new living of their own from farming. However, in many cases, this wasn't confirmed, nothing was signed for and subsequently many slaves were left to still depend on their masters to survive. I find this very sad indeed, that even after it was abolished, the slave trade still thrived in many areas.

But the act did mean that the wheels were put in motion for slaves to be free at last. Finally, hundreds of years of persecution were to come to an end and many finally began treating fellow man with the dignity he deserved, no matter of colour and creed; as an equal.

Many black people were shipped from the West Indies to work as slaves, a friend of mine had ancestors that were slaves from there and this deeply affected her. I remember if anyone ever tried to take liberties with her, she would always respond with 'slaver days are over'. I think it was a phrase she'd use in memory of her slave forefathers.

Thankfully, we are a million miles away from the slave trade these days, but no doubt how much more advanced we are as a world in which everyone should be treated as equal, there are still echoes of racism in every corner and we still have a long way on the journey of becoming united as one.

Just like the Jamaican coat of arms states:

"Out Of Many, One People"

*JJ*

## On Adoption

I know there are campaigns for mixed race and particularly black foster and adoptive parents for many reasons, which I was saying in my first column: that a child of black or mixed ethnic origin needs to know about its culture and background. Even if they can't find more black and mixed race foster and adoptive parents, the parents that are available to adopt should have the opportunity to learn about the child's heritage and culture. This knowledge can then be passed onto the child, who will know both cultures and backgrounds.

I know of a little black boy who was raised by a loving white family that did their best for him, but when asked what colour he was, he replied that he was white. The fact that he couldn't identify himself was very distressing to me. There should be resources available for people like these loving white parents who adopt a black or mixed race child to learn about their children's ethnic background. The youngsters could then be happy in their heritage and confident in both cultures. The same applies to loving black parents who adopt white children.

There are no doubt lots of children growing up with parents of a different ethnic background to themselves that can identify who they are. However, I know of one particular case where a black girl was raised by white parents who knew nothing of her origin through no fault of their own. That child grew up longing to understand her heritage and when she was old enough, she searched for answers. I question why this young woman had to put all her energy and time into finding her roots when she could have been raised with it? If we as a society are more educated about the culture of our black and mixed race children, then problems like the one occurring with this young girl will not be a future issue.

I am a white woman of today who has always mixed with another culture. The Jamaican people have taught me many qualities in life that I have passed onto my mixed race children. I have loved every minute of the Caribbean culture and still enjoy it to this day. It is a part of my life and will be until the day I die. I can therefore understand when an adopted child of mixed or other ethnic backgrounds searches for their roots and never wants to let go.

Be strong, be proud of your heritage and most of all,

be proud of who you are.

Peace and God bless,

*JJ*

## Employment and Promotion

I know the situation is getting better and our Labour government are doing what they can to prevent unfairness in the workplace, but there are still problems arising.

If you feel you have been discriminated against because of your ethnicity when applying for a job, or have been overlooked for promotion because of your ethnic origin, you have rights under the

Race Relations Act 1976.

To illustrate this point, one particular example comes to mind where an Asian gentleman, who applied for a job, was told that the position was already filled. He became suspicious and sent his friend, a white gentleman, to apply for the same position; his friend was granted an interview and later offered the job. As a result the company was scrutinised.

Although we have equal opportunities and pay in the workplace, we know that women in many circumstances earn a lower average salary than men. It is clear that women are being discriminated against, and those of ethnic origin can experience double discrimination: firstly because of their gender, and secondly their ethnicity.

**I SAY, SISTERS DON'T SUFFER IN SILENCE!**

Come forward and fight for your rights. Let this be a thing of the past, not only for now but for the next generation, our children, our grandchildren and theirs too.

Like Martin Luther King said in his speech in 1963, in which he longed for the day when 'my four children will one day live in a nation where they will not be judged by the colour of their skin but by the content of their character'.

The colour of a person's skin has no bearing on the sort of character he or she is.

In the 1970s the situation was significantly worse. I personally remember living in London and trying to make it as a model; before I found a good agent I had to 'rough it' to make ends meet so I took a job with a company who hired out wedding attire. I worked with Delroy, a Jamaican gentleman; we got on really well and worked hard. Our boss was an ignorant, feisty man who spoke to us with an attitude.

One day he spoke to Delroy with his usual bad attitude and Delroy then told him to "stuff his job" and walked out saying, "Mi nuh put up wid dis." I turned around agreeing and followed him.

These days we have more rights and don't go to work to be spoken to with disrespect. You don't have to put up with it. Most companies have employee relations to log complaints to. Although we have to respect each other, no one person is better than anybody and no person is less than anyone either.

So be strong and fight for what you believe in, but fight in the correct way, and that is with dignity, because you have rights and unless you stand up and be counted the glass ceiling will always exist.

If you feel you can relate to this column and you are suffering discrimination in the workplace, contact your nearest Citizens Advice Bureau or Racial Commissioner in your local area to challenge the problem.

God bless, take care and stand up for what you believe in.

Peace,

## JJ

## Lewis Hamilton: Racist Taunts at the Spanish Grand Prix

I was shocked and disgusted at a recent report in the press about Lewis Hamilton receiving racist taunts in Spain. I question, how many more times do we have to tolerate this racial abuse? As it's not the first time we have experienced these racist taunts: take our footballers, for example.

The handful of Spanish louts who shouted the horrific taunts to our hero need to look into the history of their ancestors. Half of Spain is descended from the Moors, a black race of Arabs who invaded Spain from North America more than a thousand years ago and gave the Spanish their culture.

I personally remember taking a holiday in Spain with a Jamaican ex-boyfriend over twenty years ago. The first week we were there we had a wonderful time; however, horror struck on the second and final week of our holiday when we met up with his Jamaican friend. We were relaxing by the pool in the hotel and a handful of Spanish men began to racially taunt my ex and his friend. Once my ex replied with dignity saying that they should look at their ancestors, the men sheepishly stopped the abuse and we went on to enjoy the rest of our holiday.

The real reason Lewis Hamilton is a hate figure in Spain is because Fernando Alonso quit McLaren for Renault as he claimed bosses favoured Hamilton. This only goes to show that it is pure jealousy from the handful of Spanish supporters and the fact he is mixed race only gives them another reason to have a go at him.

My advice to Lewis Hamilton is to keep up your amazing achievements, let no one hold you back, and the biggest revenge you can ever have is your success.

They are JEALOUS and you have everything to live for. You have made us prouder than proud and as far as your ethnic origin is concerned, you have the best of both worlds.

We Love You!!

I really hope F1 will take these racist taunts seriously; Spain could have easily been stripped of the Grand Prix. It's just a shame that the decent people of Spain have to suffer for the acts of a few.

One of my favourite songs is an old Jamaican song sung by Wayne Wade – "Black is our Colour". I believe every black man and woman should listen to this song and be proud.

Please to all our readers, God bless and take care.

*JJ*

## International Reggae Rocks

It was a busy bank holiday weekend in Cardiff city centre. People had enjoyed the sunshine and were now ready to party the night away. As the night progressed into the twilight hours, people were getting more and more excited about an international Reggae star's appearance at Q bar. The atmosphere outside the club was breath-taking due to the amount of excitement created by the multi-cultural crowd, all there to see one man – Gregory Isaacs.

The club was filled to such a capacity that some people had to be turned away. Gregory said to one of the promoters, Mr Paul Bowen, "Man gonna get a show tonight", and boy was he right!

Fans came from all over the UK. The highlight of the night was when Gregory sang "Night Nurse", one of his greatest tunes of all time. The crowd went wild and all sang along. Supporting act Live Wyya rocked the venue to fever pitch into the early hours.

I was fortunate enough to catch up with both stars as a writer for *The Big Eye News* to have a chat. They told me that they loved Cardiff and could not wait to come back as the atmosphere was electric. Both stars were supportive of *The Big Eye* newspaper and will keep a look out for it in Jamaica, where it is also read.

The last time Gregory Isaacs performed in Cardiff was twenty-five years ago at Sophia Gardens, alongside Aswad, Misty and Roots, The Specials and many more. This was a special event entitled "Rock against Racism". I believe we should have more events like this, especially in Cardiff, as it is a multi-cultural city and has been for as long as I can remember.

The one club that sticks in my mind was called Casablanca and was located in Cardiff Bay. As Casablanca played some of the best Reggae and Ska music around, people travelled from all over the UK to enjoy a night out there. Unfortunately, the club is now closed even though they had a reunion this April. It would be wonderful if they could reopen.

We can also look forward to Sanchez and many more Jamaican artists coming to Cardiff, and if we're lucky enough Gregory Isaacs and Live Wyya will come back too.

I remember going to see John Holt in the club Top Rank in Cardiff city around thirty years ago. He had an orchestra playing while he sang hits like "The Further You Look", "Mr Bojangles" and many more. John Holt is still a music legend to this day. One of his greatest tracks is called "Out of My Mind", where he sings "You've Got Me Going" and buoy I better say bye for now coz me ah get goin talking about all dis music!

Until next month, peace and chill of your music.

Love and God bless,

*JJ*

**P.S.** - I dedicate this column to an old friend of mine, Paul Wickens, who grew up in a predominantly white area and idolised Gregory Isaacs all his life; he also owns every one of his records.

## Bullying

There is no place in our society for bullies. They are insecure cowards who prey on vulnerable people for whatever excuse they can find. Bullying can be triggered by a number of factors: if a person is over- or underweight, race, being too bright or not bright enough in class… the list goes on, you just cannot win.

YES YOU CAN!

We cannot allow bullies to get away with the torture they put their victims through, and telling someone you are being bullied will put an end to it.

I was shocked to learn our very own undefeated boxing champion Joe Calzaghe admitted to being bullied when he was at school. Joe Calzaghe is of mixed race origin, from a Welsh mother and a Sardinian father, who has now retired from boxing undefeated. We are all so proud of him.

I hope when he talks about being bullied it will influence many people who are victims of bullying and give them the courage to come forward and speak out as they know that someone like Joe Calzaghe has been in the same predicament as them and look at him now; it just goes to show that:

SUCCESS IS THE BEST FORM OF REVENGE!

No matter how big or small the success, it demonstrates your willingness to rise above the bully.

I remember my child experienced a bullying incident during her time at school. There was an occasion where another girl kept throwing chewing gum at her from the desk behind. As a concerned parent I asked my child if she wanted me to get involved and report it to the school. She immediately became frightened at the mention of this and told me that if I did, she would never tell me anything again.

I had to do something, whilst respecting my daughter's wishes, so I decided to meet my child after school one day and walk home instead of catching the bus. We walked and caught up with the bully, who was also walking home. She looked at my daughter and I said to her in the roughest voice I could fake, "Alright?" The girl stuttered, "Yes." That was all I did – nothing against any laws or rules, I just merely made an appearance.

The next day the bully was intrigued who the person was walking with my daughter and asked her who I was. "My mother," my daughter replied, and from that day the bullying stopped.

The appearance I made showed the bully that my daughter had someone, and that someone was me, her mother. I also kept my promise to my daughter and never mentioned the chewing gum incident.

Not all approaches like this work, but it worked for me.

It is difficult to encourage our children to talk to us about bullying, but as a parent/guardian we can sense something is wrong and sometimes we have to be patient and wait for them to talk to us.

Unfortunately, for some people, it is too late. The alarming facts show that bullying can drive people to suicide. What bullies should realise is that it is someone's loved ones they are bullying, and that they will get caught out in the end.

I know there have been many awareness campaigns highlighting the effects of bullying and it is good to see schools including this topic in their curriculum, because it can ruin people's lives.

Come on, don't be ashamed, speak to someone you trust and believe me, it will stop. Remember, if it can happen to our champ, Joe Calzaghe, it can happen to anyone!

Don't hide and shelter the bully, speak out and tell someone.

Take care,

*JJ*

## Sus Law? Red Card Against Racism

I was shocked and upset at reports that one of our Premier League footballers and a friend were harassed by police as they looked in a jeweller's window in Cheshire. The twenty-year-old Everton striker Victor Anichebe was window-shopping with a friend when police officers pounced.

After a heated row, Victor Anichebe's friend was handcuffed, which later the police admitted was an overreaction and apologised to the pair, who were distressed by the incident but were happy to let it go.

I felt so sorry for them. He may have been window-shopping, but as you can imagine he could most probably have bought the shop! But that's beside the point.

I remember living in London in the late 1970s when the Sus Law was rife. Where police had the power to stop and search anybody they 'sussed' was going to commit a crime, as if they could magically read people's minds.

This caused a great deal of stress to my Jamaican boyfriend of the time and myself. When we would go out to many parts of London shopping, to the cinema or for a glass of wine on a nice summer's day, they could stop him. I found it very difficult at that time to be in a mixed race relationship.

The police even came round to our house one day looking for my boyfriend; by this time I had had enough. I told them he wasn't in as I knew he had done nothing wrong. They heard a noise upstairs, which I explained was the dog. As they questioned me, my boyfriend ran out of the house as we had had enough of the constant questioning and interrogation for crimes he had never committed, but I suppose being Jamaican he must have been 'thinking' about a crime in their eyes!

They always seemed to stop young black and mixed race men around that time. A cousin of mine, who was a young white man, came and stayed with us for a while and when I walked round London with him, we did not have the issue of being stopped.

Don't get me wrong, I will give credit where credit is due and even my ex-boyfriend would say that the British Police would always catch dangerous and evil criminals in the end. But to pick on an innocent person just because of the colour of their skin due to the Sus Law was unacceptable. However, that was the attitude of the law in the 1970s; thankfully, the law was abolished. The story of the Everton footballer reminded me of the times in the 70s and brought back the memories of what we went through with the Sus Law. It is good to see that the police apologised to Anichebe and his friend as it shows that times have changed in mixed race Britain.

*JJ*

**P.S.**

Talking about the 70s, I bought the film "The Harder They Come" by Jimmy Cliff with his greatest hits "Many Rivers to Cross", "You Can

Get It If You Really Want" and, of course, "The Harder They Come". What a film, wicked!!

## Skin Bleaching and Sunbeds

I read with great interest and astonishment in November's issue of *The Big Eye* on skin bleaching creams, "Ethnic Identity Crisis". As you all know my issues are mainly focused on mixed race and to be proud of who you are.

Firstly, I would like to say that black skin is beautiful and the thought of anyone trying to lighten it with creams, especially bleaching creams, horrifies me.

In Jamaica, health authorities say hundreds of people are skin bleaching and the problem is that many people misuse skin lightening creams, which are prescribed at low doses to correct uneven pigmentation. The majority of white women would love to have darker skin, and although I am preaching to you, we do the same as what you are doing. We use sunbeds which are dangerous in the long term. In addition to this we use tanning creams which penetrate deep into the pigment of the skin, which make us go darker temporarily. So it seems none of us are really happy with our skin tone. Many white women would agree with me that darker skin is beautiful, and I for one admit to using sunbeds over the years and paying the price for it when I developed a cancerous spot on my face. Thankfully it was removed successfully. At the time I was extremely worried and will never use a sunbed again. This goes to show that both black and white women go through the same problems. Instead of using dangerous methods, there are other alternatives such as make-ups and moisturisers which can add a little tone to our lighter or darker skin without transforming it completely and losing our identity.

As previously stated in my first column, a little girl of nine years of age and of mixed race origin who grew up in a predominantly white environment had a problem with her skin tone and began scrubbing her skin with bleach; not bleaching creams, which are harmful enough: it was Domestos bleach, which can be fatal. Her mother was heartbroken and I advised the mother to tell the child how beautiful she was; now she is confident and happy with her appearance.

Take Alexander Dunn, for example, a successful Welsh model and actress, who admits she would love to have darker skin but is proud and confident in her appearance. She has a beautiful nine-year-old, mixed race child. She has raised her child to be proud and confident of her culture and recently while Alex was creaming her little girl's skin the girl suddenly said, "Mum, please don't clean my brown skin away."

This goes to show that the confidence that you instil as a parent into your child can have a positive effect on your child's well-being and confidence in life. It's a far cry from the little girl I once helped.

We live in a society where people can be judgmental, and even though we do not want to create problems where none exist regarding skin tone, I feel we have to be on our guard because racism is a light sleeper. In life, if we are prepared for what is thrown at us then we can cope with anything and rise above this negativity such as racism and remember we should learn to "Love the skin we're in".

Peace and God bless,

*JJ*

## 'A' Level Exam Result Nightmare

As a parent, August is a time when 'A' Level results can determine your son or daughter's future. It is normally a time of joy and happiness or a time to consider other options to create the best future for them. It is not a time when parents and children should be traumatised and grief-stricken for errors created by exam boards' and schools' incompetence.

I personally went through hell last month as my daughter's 'A' Level Certificate was lost and my son's GCSE results were mixed up with another boy with the same name. I have got some vital advice for parents this month to check their children's exams militantly.

It is difficult in this day and age to raise children, especially from a broken home and a mixed race background, as a single parent, without having the worry of mistakes caused by schools.

It was a Thursday morning on 'A' Level results day. My daughter and I arrived at the school early, eager to know if she had done enough hard work to pass her 'A' Levels to go to the university of her choice. As I waited anxiously in my car for her to come out many thoughts were running through my head, but I would never have thought that what was about to happen ever could!

She came out of the school informing me that she had passed her 'A' Levels but one of the certificates was lost! At the time it didn't seem to matter as we assumed that as long as the system stated she had passed, she could go to university. I rang the university to inform them and they told us that without that certificate they could not accept her. When I received this news, the next two weeks became one of the most stressful and testing ordeals of my life. It has been my daughter's dream to go to university and I have struggled for years to provide for her future. The struggle is not just financial, but encouraging her by telling her that if she is going to make it, she will do so through the education system, and that education is the key to a successful life.

I fought and fought for my daughter's rights; it was two weeks of agony. At one point I told the school that I was not leaving until the problem was solved. It was extremely difficult when one of the teachers who lost the certificate told me: "Can't you accept it, Ms Jones, that your daughter is NOT going to university, she has failed?"

I started sobbing on the phone but this just made me stronger to prove that my daughter had passed her exams and that she could go to university.

I kept a log of my feelings throughout the ordeal and have illustrated some of the quotes I was feeling at the time below.

**Results day 21st August** – my daughter has passed her 'A' Levels and achieved the grades for her first-choice university. I am so proud of her. I rang the university and even though she has passed, we need the certificates as proof otherwise her place will be taken up. This is the very certificate that has been lost!! It's bank holiday weekend, we haven't time on our side. I've just got to hope there is light at the end of the tunnel!

**26th August** – Didn't sleep all night, feel ill with worry. I rang the school first thing and after an upsetting discussion about their incompetence I said that if the work is not found I will take this further.

**27th August** – Get up early, haven't slept all night. On the way to the school, feeling absolutely shattered and distraught. After a meeting with the teachers, I demanded that they sort it and they confirmed it was a clerical error. They apologised for the trauma and grief they have caused. That is not good enough; I wanted the qualification they lost and my child deserved.

**28th August** – Preparing to go up to the school again. I'm at the end of my tether now. I feel I'm going to have a breakdown. I'm not coming out of the school until this is sorted. Teacher explained he will ring the university and explain that my daughter had passed and that it was an error on the school's part.

The university lecturer even rang my daughter to stress that she had done nothing wrong and it is not her fault.

Waiting for the school to ring the lecturer to confirm it was a clerical error is like waiting on a time bomb. I can't sleep, eat, it has taken all my strength but I have to keep fighting for my daughter's future.

I received a phone call later that day to find out that the university had accepted her. We both broke down in tears together, so happy and relieved that she has finally got what she deserved and, readers, it is only because I stood up and fought for her rights. My advice to parents is never give up, whatever obstacles you face in life. Regarding my children, I can deal with anything. My advice to our black and mixed race children: let nothing and no-one hold you back, just follow your dreams and be proud of who you are.

As you know, readers, I love my Reggae music as it reminds me of the strength and influence the Jamaican people have over me, which I am very proud of. I would like to thank Itana as I bought her CD during this difficult time and playing it gave me inner strength. She has the most powerful female voice I have ever heard and I give thanks to her. I truly believe her album has the potential to be a worldwide No 1 seller.

Peace and God bless and stand up for your rights,

*JJ*

**Further advice for parents**

There are schemes across the country such as the National Black Boys Can Association based in South East London, which works with city organisations including J.P Morgan and mentors young, black students from all backgrounds. To date, 142 students have participated in the programme, which aims to boost academic and leadership skills. As a result, their GCSE results are soaring. The Black Boys Can Association runs projects across the country in areas including Birmingham and London for boys aged 9 to 16 for a fee of £3.00. What I personally find interesting is that they learn about black history, which they do not teach enough of in our schools, but should. They also help with anger management issues. I only wish I had known this a few years ago as I would have most certainly have encouraged my son to join.

## Barack Obama

As you all know, I feel passionate about our black and mixed race society. I always try to give hope to those lucky children who are of mixed race heritage, because they have the best of both worlds. I encourage readers to be proud of who they are and to follow their dreams, because to have more than one blood running through your veins is a special gift. Therefore, what better individual to discuss in this column, who is an inspiring role model to us all, than Barack Obama.

Barack Obama is running for President of the United States of America. If he wins, he will be the first black president of the USA. There is no doubt in my mind that he is the man for the job and will make America proud, and we and many other countries will benefit. The reason he will make us proud is that he will favour no one race but all races, because like my own two children he is the son of a black man and a white woman and has been raised to respect all cultures. He was also raised with the help of his white grandfather, who survived World War II, and a grandmother who worked on a bomber assembly line, just like my own mother who worked in an ammunitions factory during the war.

I truly believe he is finishing off Martin Luther King's work!!

I would also like to pay tribute to Cardiff's own rising star, Vaughan Gething. Vaughan, a member of GMB's Cardiff and District Branch, has become the first youngest black president of the TUC Wales. This illustrates the big changes in waves in our society. Thirty-four-year-old Vaughan has been an active trade unionist and politician, once holding the Butetown Ward seat on Cardiff City Council for Labour.

I know that Vaughan is a man of many talents and has the same political stance and values as Barack Obama. I also believe he is our version of him, as they are both young, handsome, black politicians, and I feel they both have the power to bring both nations together as one.

The GMB Union walked away with the first TUC equality award. This is evidence that the GMB Wales Region is actively promoting racial equality. This highlights to me that this is the union for black, mixed race, ethnic and individuals of all races in the workplace to join and become part of.

I would also like to congratulate my sister Jill for winning the 2008 Wales TUC equality award. She has organised and facilitated equal pay campaigns, on a local, regional and international level. She works by supporting women who have suffered from domestic and racial abuse. Due to her sheer determination, Jill has also succeeded in securing support and funding from Welsh Assembly Ministers.

As sisters, we share a passion for our black and mixed race Britain. Like myself, Jill loves Jamaican food, Reggae music, the culture and the people. Jill has done a wonderful job helping others achieve their rights; keep up the good work, Jill.

Peace and God bless,

*JJ*

**P.S.** - Since writing this column, Barack Obama has become president of the United States of America.

## Nursing Homes

How would you feel if at a young age you emigrated to a foreign country, leaving your family and friends behind in the hope of a better life? During your time there you worked hard and prospered, assisting the country's economy and proudly influencing others about your culture and maintaining your values. Then, imagine you are at an age where you need care within a residential home and the moment you go into care your cultural needs regarding the food you have always loved are not catered for.

This is what is happening to our Jamaican people within the UK.

Our Jamaican people came to the UK from the 1940s as the *Windrush* boat sailed into Britain's harbours in 1948. They made a new life, worked hard and prospered, helping this country's economy. Although they lived and worked in this country they always maintained their Jamaican culture, enjoyed their own house parties, Reggae and Ska music, food etc.

It saddens me that while this country owes them a great deal, when some retire into nursing homes they are not catered for when it comes to their Jamaican cuisine. Jamaicans in this country should not have to stop eating the food they were brought up on and love so dearly. Food such as ackee and salt fish, curry goat, brown stew chicken, steam fish, rice n' peas... I could go on listing these delicious cuisines.

I'm sure our Labour government would look into this atrocity if it were put forward to them. I am personally going to put this issue forward to the government and will let you know the outcome in a future column.

When this problem was highlighted to me I became very annoyed, as I imagined the anguish I would feel if a member of my family were taken into care and did not have the food provided for them that they had always been accustomed to. This must be happening to many Jamaican families in the UK today. On an even more depressing note, what about the elderly Jamaican people who have no family and cannot benefit from their loved ones who would cook and carry it in for them?

My children were born in this country and are of mixed race heritage and have had a heavy Jamaican influence as far as their music, food and culture is concerned. It is incredibly important to me as a mother for them to embrace this culture. Most of my life I have mixed with Jamaican people, whom I love and respect very much indeed. It breaks my heart at the thought of the Jamaican people who retire into nursing homes and have to stop living the way they used to.

It is something we all need to think about and take seriously.

Normally I write about mixed race issues, what I know and what I have experienced. It is the experience which has given me my knowledge. I feel so strongly about this issue that I have to speak out about it and do something.

So before I leave you for another month, imagine one more thing. The next time you cook a wonderful Jamaican dish, think about these elderly Jamaicans and how much they are missing out and if it were you, how would you feel?

As I have stated, I will be dealing with this accordingly with the government.

Until then,

Peace, take care and stand up for your rights.

## *JJ*

**P.S.** - As you may know, Reggae music plays a big part in my life so I could not miss the opportunity of interviewing the one and only, Reggae mega star Horace Andy.

Horace rocked Bristol Carling Academy on Thursday 13th November. He carries a multi-cultural crowd wherever he performs in Europe. I was overwhelmed by the variety of different cultures and nationalities at the performance; it was amazing.

When he sang one of his all-time greats, "Sky Larking", the crowd erupted. It was so breath-taking, the crowd were screaming for more! I told him the vibe I was feeling and he gracefully replied that this is the atmosphere he is used to and it made him so happy.

## HMS *Windrush*

In 1948, the HMS *Windrush* sailed into Britain from Jamaica bringing hundreds of Jamaicans to start a new life in the UK.

They settled all over Britain in cities such as London, Manchester, Bristol, Cardiff, Liverpool, Birmingham and many more. They found jobs in hospitals, on railways, buses, anywhere there was work available and worked hard and settled in to their new lives in this very different world to them.

They were an industrious lot, yet some found it hard to cope, but persevered anyway despite the enormous prejudice set against them, especially when looking for properties to rent. Constantly, everywhere they went, they would be greeted with signs stating 'NO BLACKS' and would be turned away merely because of the colour of their skin. Imagine how this must have felt.

This could never happen in this day of age as we have become more educated, more accepting of fellow man, no matter their colour or religion. Imagine the uproar now if a landlord openly refused tenancy to a black man? It simply wouldn't happen and it's a credit to the way we've progressed as people.

I must stress, that despite the overwhelming prejudice back then, it wasn't everyone who treated black people this way. There were some people who embraced them and made them feel welcome in their new home, a home in which they worked hard and contributed to the economy as much as anyone else.

Many of those Jamaicans brought their children with them and many gave birth when they were here which made their children British. It was then this generation that integrated more with British men and women, and it's our children today who are integrating even more. With every passing generation we become more as one and more races come together to make our country an ever growing melting pot. I believe that one day the majority of people in this country will be of mixed race.

The canvass of Britain today is very much different from years gone by. On every street corner, on every train, in every park we see people of mixed race relationships and we don't bat an eyelid. Take yourself back to the times before and imagine the same scene, it would be one of disbelief, unheard of. If looks could kill, then I would have been dead a long time ago!

Myself and my partner would walk down the street together and have to endure shouts of shocking racial abuse, we'd be targeted openly in public and be addressed in all kinds of racial slurs. But I would always rise above it, and console myself that these uneducated, un-accepting and ignorant people should be felt sorry for because they thought love couldn't exist between two people of different colour. If people acted the way now that they did in the 1970s, then they would be arrested for such vile and obtrusive behaviour, for this I'm eternally glad.

My ex-boyfriend was one of those sent for by their parents who had come to this country. I remember him telling me that when he arrived here and travelled by train from Victoria Station, he was intrigued by the smoking chimneys he passed on the way. He remarked to his sister, "Oh look, there are lots of bakeries in England," not realising it was the norm here to have burning fires to keep our houses warm. He was soon to learn that England was a lot colder than back in Jamaica where the only smoke to come out of chimneys was indeed in bakeries. This was over four decades ago.

My children's grandmother came to this country from the West Indies many years ago when she was just 16 years of age. She came to the UK on a government scheme to be a nurse and was offered the opportunity to live and work in the place of her choice. She chose Wales, despite others in her group opting for more predictable destinations like London or Birmingham.

She settled well in Wales, but did greatly miss her mother as anyone would. But she fought it out, and stayed on to become a qualified nurse and spent her entire working life in local hospitals in the Welsh Valleys before retiring. Not long after passing out as a nurse, she met her husband to be, my children's grandfather.

He was a patient in the hospital where she worked. She nursed him and fell in love with him at the same time. What was unusual about this, at the time, was that this love existed between her, a West Indian woman, and him, a local Welsh miner. Proof again that love knows no colour, even back in the days where this would be scorned at by many.

She gave many years of great service to the nursing industry here in Wales, and we thank the foresight of the government of that time for making this happen. We should be thankful as a nation to the service of women like her and very proud of how accepting we became.

The same goes to all those who sailed into the UK aboard the HMS *Windrush* all those years ago. This influx was the seed of the plant of acceptance that was soon to blossom many years later by a country that would grow to welcome and treat fellow humans as simply that; fellow humans. They worked hard for our country that was to become 'their country' as well, making a fantastic contribution to our society as a whole.

## *JJ*

## Melting Pot

Mixed race is not just about black and white!

For instance, mixed race could be white British mixed with white Polish, black Portuguese mixed with Jamaican or black African mixed with white German and so on.

Our world is a 'Melting Pot', as the Blue Mink song goes. In other words, cultures today from all over the world are creating relationships which are broadening our mixed race society. To highlight this point there are a number of European workers who emigrate to Britain to work and prosper. There are a number of Polish people who have come to Britain to work and have settled into relationships with a variety of nationalities in Britain.

I have a Polish friend who is in a relationship with a Jamaican man. It's so nice to see them sharing each other's culture. There are always delicious Jamaican meals being cooked, and Polish dishes too. They also share the love of each other's music; it's wonderful to witness.

I am aware that there are a minority of people who criticise the Polish people living in Britain. A family member was campaigning for the Labour government when she was approached by a member of the public challenging her about the Polish living in Britain.

His argument was that the Polish people were taking his 'jobs'. The politician's reply was, "There are a number of Polish people who work hard in slaughter houses. Would you work there, sir?"

The gentleman's response was, "No."

I would like to remind the minority of people who share this opinion that the Polish people helped Britain win the war in 1944. The Prime Minister at that time, Sir Winston Churchill, made it clear that the Polish people are welcome in Britain forever more, for what they did for our country. It is a coincidence that the Polish people are integrating with the British public; it is like it was meant to be.

Five decades on from 1944, there is a small community of Polish people living in the south-west of England. Many who survived the war are still there to this day; they have their own family history in the country and have developed a peaceful community integrating their wonderful culture within Britain. They have their own grocery, coffee and gift shops.

If more British people were aware of this history they would not be so hard on the Polish people. One way to incorporate this would be through the use of a television documentary on how the Polish helped Britain win the war. Wider publicity on this history would help stamp out racism against them. As I have stated before, we must be on our guard because racism is a light sleeper, so let us not tolerate it.

Take care until next month,

*JJ*

I would like to pay tribute to a local businessman and friend, Alan Jones aka Bronco, who sadly passed away in January 2009.

He was a young fifty-five-year-old, a man of courage and determination who mixed with all cultures. He loved to travel; his real love was India. His other passions were music and sport, especially boxing and football.

He was a dedicated fan of Cardiff City Football Club and was a well-known and respected man within our town and inner cities. He introduced the height of fashion to our town, a man of true style.

My son worked for him, in his designer clothing shop. I am grateful for his strong values, discipline, self-respect and above all his refusal to worry about people's idle gossip and belief in rising above any obstacles that life throws at you.

Raising a son as a single parent is hard, and I always hoped someone would be there to talk to and guide my son. Bronco was that someone.

Without even knowing it, he meant the world to me.

Rest in peace, Bronco.

*JJ*

## Too White To Be His!

As you know, I raised the issue of mixed race children living in a predominantly white environment and how they should cope if problems arise. In other words, don't sit there and say nothing: there is help and advice out there. I, for one, would be happy to help and give advice to parents.

It was very interesting to read August/September's issue of *The Big Eye* (Pete Hanniford) on self-actualisation, because not only have I raised two children of mixed ethnic origin as a single parent, I have nurtured and encouraged them in their education. The fact that my daughter is applying to study at university makes me feel extremely proud. I believe that education is the key to a good life and all children have this chance, and Pete Hanniford is right in saying that it is important that both parents are part of a child's life. If both parents cannot be a part of that child's life, then one parent is better than two that don't get on: there is nothing worse than a child seeing their parents at war all the time. Nurturing and encouraging your child at school doesn't cost anything, and the more praise a child gets from a parent, the more they will learn.

Going back to the mixed race issue, I was very upset a few years ago when a celebrity had a mixed race child with a premiership footballer. Not only did the father abandon them while she was pregnant, leaving her with the ordeal of going through the birth alone, when the baby was born he made the ridiculous remark that the baby was "too white" to be his! I was furious when I read this statement, because one of my two children was also born white. He went darker in time, just like this celebrity's child. It does not mean that if the child was born white, that it is not this particular person's child, because it can take more of one parent's genes. There are cases of twins born of mixed race origin where one child is white and the other black, therefore this particular footballer's statement was absurd and ignorant, as it turned out that the child was definitely his.

My topic is mixed race society, but I call on all races, all "God's children" to be proud of their heritage. As I always say, be strong, be confident and be proud of who you are, because even at times of dullness and despair, always remember you have the best of both worlds.

*JJ*

## Embrace Your Culture

As you know, I discuss mixed race issues and how to be strong. A typical influential character is Mel B of the Spice Girls, who grew up in a mixed race family. She is confident, strong and very proud of her mixed race origin. Growing up, she always referred to her two grandmothers as her "Black Nan" and her "White Nan" (talk about the best of both worlds!). She is happy and confident in both cultures. Her confidence was instilled by her understanding of both cultures and is an inspirational example for the many mixed race children and families of today.

Many years ago it was frowned upon to bear a child out of wedlock. One particular incident remains in my mind, of a white woman who had a baby with a black American GI. He returned to America and left the woman to have the baby alone as a single parent. Soon after, her family disowned her.

When the baby was born she gave him up for adoption through the stress and pressure of the situation. She never stopped thinking of the child, but went on to marry a white man and have a family with him.

When her first child was an adult, mother and child had a reunion. She could not bond with her child; the child was heartbroken. They did try to keep in contact, but it failed.

Sometimes we all have things in life that upset and bother us, but we have to be strong and **CAN** think positive and turn our lives around. There is one thing that can be said about the British public: they like to see people turn their lives around. It takes courage to recognise and admit you are in the wrong, and to do something about it. As Kelly Chin wrote in her column (October issue): "No matter the chatter, hold your head up." I couldn't agree with her more; she made me feel a sense of strength.

I regard myself as a strong woman, but I also have weaknesses like everybody else. I thank the Jamaican people for teaching me strong values in life, which I have passed on to my mixed race children.

As I have stated in my previous column, I lived in Kingston, Jamaica, and I miss it so much, especially Elsher beach on a Sunday morning for 'fried fish and festival'. I have travelled to many cities in the UK and wish there were more Caribbean restaurants in the city centres. I always seem to have to travel a little out of the city to find one. I think they would do so well in every city centre. The food is so delicious and healthy.

The problem is that once you find one, you don't want to leave. With the Reggae music, the atmosphere, the food – not to mention the rum punch! – you're in paradise.

Until next time,

Peace, chill out and take care.

*JJ*

## A Wake-up Call

'Jade's legacy' has echoed throughout the country during the past few weeks due to the devastating news that Jade Goody's life is sadly coming to an end as a result of cervical cancer.

'Jade's legacy' has enabled women to become more aware of cervical cancer and the importance of going for regular smear tests. Not only that, but her legacy has also caused parliament to rethink its smear test age restriction and allowed women to get tested from the age of twenty instead of twenty-five.

I, for one, have always had regular smear tests, but for some reason I am two years late. However, when I heard the upsetting news about Jade Goody, I immediately booked one. Jade Goody, who comes from a mixed race background, has been in and out of the news spotlight for some time, and has received some criticism for what has been called racist remarks to Shilpa Shetty on television. However, she has learned from her mistakes and was starring in the latest version of Celebrity Big Brother in India, which was hosted by Shilpa Shetty, when she was diagnosed with the disease. Jade has become close friends with Shilpa Shetty since then, and Shilpa Shetty wanted to visit Jade before she dies.

Jade Goody has always been honest about allowing the cameras to film her illness. She made it clear she was doing it for her son's future, so that they would have enough money to live the life she never had. Who can begrudge her that? To die so young and leave two little boys is heart-breaking enough, and I know that no amount of money can compensate for your mother.

This dreadful, dreadful illness which has struck Jade is not only a wake-up call for women, but I feel it is also a wake-up call for parents to think of their children's future.

I have always prayed when my children were young and even now that I would live long enough to see them through. Yes, I admit I have always worried about leaving them provided for financially because I, like many other parents, spend and treat our children to every penny we've got. If I had tried saving when my children were young I wouldn't have been able to treat them to holidays, cinema and buying them good food and clothing.

I am always interested in Pete Hanniford's columns in *The Big Eye* and find it helpful when he encourages us to "put something away for a rainy day".

If I am honest, I haven't.

This is a wake-up call even now that my children are teenagers. I shudder to think that leaving them in this world without me is dreadful enough, but to leave them with no financial security scares me. Even if we are not in a position to save for our children's future, we should seriously think about taking out policies so that if anything should happen to us our children are provided for.

I know I am; it's never too late.

Hearts go out to Jade from all over the world including Mel B,

Michael Jackson, Oprah Winfrey and so many more. Her legacy has made us all think about our health and our family's future.

God bless,

*JJ*

## Most Beautiful Black Woman Competition

I would like to congratulate our Most Beautiful Black Woman in Britain winner, Patrice from Bristol. She truly is beautiful, even more so in real life. I think she has the potential to be Britain's next supermodel. Recently I had the privilege to meet up with her and the gorgeous runners-up, Juanita and Elaine. It must have been an extremely tough competition to decide a winner from all the girls who competed as they were all stunners.

As I have stated in a previous column, I have travelled to many cities in the UK and wish there were more Caribbean restaurants in the city centres because there seem to be few around where people can experience a taste of Caribbean culture. I always had to travel way out of the city to find one, but NOT ANY MORE!!

At the weekend I met up with *The Big Eye* at a stunning Caribbean restaurant called Xamayca, Bristol Street, Birmingham. The food was so delicious that once you were in there you did not want to leave.

I also recently visited Mr Jerk's Caribbean restaurant in the heart of central London, Wardour Street, which was amazing too. I caught up and had a chat with the owner. He agreed that the reasons I gave about the lack of Caribbean restaurants in the city were his exact reasons for opening a Caribbean restaurant in the city in the first place, as years ago we would struggle to find one. I think they would do so well all over Britain; the Caribbean food is so delicious and healthy.

I have cooked Caribbean dishes most of my life but it was whilst living in Kingston, Jamaica, that I cooked it to 'perfection'. I thank the Jamaican people for teaching me strong values in life, which I pass on to my mixed race children.

When I ate at these restaurants, it was encouraging to note that there was an array of different cultures experiencing the wonderful Caribbean food. It's good to know that all races are enjoying the Caribbean food – and what a wonderful way to promote the Caribbean culture, through delicious curry goat, oxtail, ackee & salt fish and so many more.

Anyway, that's enough about food – "Me ah get hungry".

Peace, take care and God bless,

*JJ*

## Race Row

In February, a race row erupted, when black councillor Shirley Brown, Bristol's first black Lib Dem Councillor, called her Indian counterpart "a coconut" during a council debate. MP Shirley Brown made the jibe at the Bristol City Council meeting. The slur was directed at Conservative Jay Jethwa, when she proposed funding cuts for an inner-city equality group's plan to spend £750,000 on teaching slave history.

Mrs Jethwa feels that it was racially related and told the meeting, "spending £750,000 of taxpayer's money righting the wrongs of slavery did not make sense". I feel it's important to teach all our children about slavery; MP Mrs Brown stated what she was really saying was like coconut water, you can either take it or throw it away. She also said that she wanted Mrs Jethwa to know she was throwing away her comments.

Mrs Brown has since sent a letter of apology to Mrs Jethwa. I personally don't believe Mrs Brown is racist as they are trying to make out. It was merely a slip of the tongue, and a mistake. I don't believe she is racist, just as I don't believe Jade Goody was racist.

Jade Goody is mixed race. I am not condoning her row with Shilpa Shetty in the Big Brother house in 2007 at all; Jade made some mistakes like us all and she couldn't apologise enough. Shilpa Shetty became close friends with Jade, wanting to make a last visit from her Indian home to see Jade for the last time before she died. Jade was even starring on India's version of Celebrity Big Brother, which was hosted by Shilpa herself, when she was told in the diary room that she had cervical cancer last August; at this stage she was given a chance of survival, but then sadly her cancer spread quickly and she died. She is not remembered as racist by the general public.

I for one will stand up for anyone being racially abused, and sometimes things are said with no intention to offend, but we all should know right and wrong in what we say, not to offend one another in any shape or form.

*JJ*

## The System's Not Always Right - Julie Jones 18/11/09

It seems dramas keep coming my way, but they are not in vain, because what I'm about to tell you there are lessons to be learnt from, and it will give encouragement to others to fight for their rights.

On 9th June 2009, I was travelling on a busy dual-carriageway on a leisure drive with a friend of mine when a police car followed me with its sirens on, indicating to me to pull over, which I did. He asked me to provide my insurance certificate, which was in the boot of the car at the time, so I told the police officer that I would look for it. It took a while to find, as the boot was full of shopping and my daughter's things as she was changing universities at the time.

The officer also had a form which stated to tick what ethnicity you are. He looked at me and asked me what I classed myself as and before I could answer, he ticked 'White'. I was shocked, because you don't legally have to answer that question. I also told him I have Spanish in my family, so I could have ticked mixed race for all he knew; how dare he make that assumption?

I eventually found the certificate, but only after pulling all my things out onto the roadside, as the officer was being very awkward indeed. I explained to him that I was driving the vehicle on a trader's insurance certificate, but he didn't believe me. I told him that if he doubted my word, then he can easily ring the person who was the policyholder to validate my story.

I rang the policyholder and put the officer on with him. The officer was extremely rude, uttering closed statements such as "you're not listening to me" over and over again. It was an embarrassing situation to be in, so I then rang the insurance broker, who advised me over the phone that I was indeed insured and I had nothing to worry about. The broker asked me to put him on with the police officer to explain that everything was in order. I passed the phone to the officer; we were both sat in the car at the time, and all of a sudden the officer asked me to leave the car as he wanted to have "a private conversation".

I was shocked, and as I waited outside of the car for him, all I could think about was why is he keeping me outside of the car like this? What discussion is going on in there that he clearly doesn't want me privy to?

My friend and I stood outside the car for several minutes. Eventually, I opened the police car door and asked him how long he was going to be. He totally ignored me. So I waited again. I then opened the door to ask again; this was getting ridiculous. But this time, he got angry and locked me out of the police car, leaving my friend and me standing on the side of a very busy road. I understand police can lock you inside a police car, but to lock themselves in away from me baffled me.

When the 'private conversation' was over, for some very strange reason I wasn't insured. This despite the very same broker initially telling me that I was. The police officer had told the broker a completely different story to what I had told him because on a trader's policy, there are certain rules.

I couldn't believe what I was witnessing, and my friend shared this disbelief at what had happened. This police officer had intentionally manipulated my story and changed it in a way to make it look like I was in the wrong. The officer ordered a recovery vehicle to take my car to a compound and kept repeating to me the words "I'll see you in court" in a sarcastic manner, as if he were trying to inflame the situation further.

At first I accepted defeat. I thought, what chance have I got? This is a police officer after all; it would be like a David versus Goliath battle. But I evaluated the situation and knew deep down in my heart that he was wrong, and that I shouldn't stand for this.

Later that day I went to my local police station with exactly the same insurance certificate, which they accepted as proof of my insurance and allowed me to go and pick the car up, albeit after I had paid the £154 charge.

I could not believe the hypocrisy; all of a sudden the same certificate which I had produced earlier and was declined as invalid was now fine in the eyes of the law that had seen fit to impound my car previously that day. I knew now that I could not allow this police officer to get away with what he had done to me, for fear he would keep on doing the same to other people. It was not right, and my battle began.

First of all, there is no way in this day and age you can get away with driving without insurance; if you get pulled over, then that's it. But if you've not done anything wrong, don't sit back and let things pass – stand up for yourself and fight your case.

So I put in a formal complaint against the officer, and even the headquarters I rang to lodge this complaint said that he was wrong to lock me out of the police car and that it just didn't sound right. They told me the complaint would have to be put in writing, so I typed it up.

In the meantime, I had a court date coming up, so I sent the form back to the court pleading 'not guilty'. During this time, because I had made an official complaint against the police officer, I received a call from a liaison officer who would try to resolve the dispute. He called to my house and informed me that he had spoken to the officer involved and had identified that he had made three errors.

Firstly, why didn't he have the audio on in the police car? Why wasn't I present when he spoke to the insurance broker? And why did he lock me out of the car?

The liaison officer asked me if I wanted to end the complaint there and then as he had addressed the errors made, but I replied no, definitely not, as I'd rather wait until the court case is over before I decide.

The court date arrived and I was, understandably, very nervous, as most people would be in such a formal legal situation. I appeared in front of the judge and pleaded not guilty to the charges. The prosecutor explained to me that the insurance certificate I showed to the police officer was acceptable but I needed to bring a covering letter from the trader and she would dismiss the case. The hearing was adjourned for two weeks.

Two weeks later I again appeared in court with the letter, only to find a completely different atmosphere and a different prosecutor, who appeared very nervous, and wouldn't accept my covering letter. I was shocked. The clerk was very rude to me and bordering on aggressive, and the judge then told me I would have to return the following day with my driver's licence.

A solicitor later informed me that I was unfortunate as I had a very inexperienced prosecutor, but that's not fair, I thought, that shouldn't go against me. I understand you can have good and bad luck determining your evening at, say, a bingo hall, but in a court of law? This was preposterous.

From going from being told two weeks ago that the case was just a formality and all I needed to clear my name was to bring in the covering letter, to my case hanging on a thread due to the inexperience of the prosecutor was a substantial shift in occurrence that threatened my chances of success unfairly. I was a letter away from having the case dismissed, but no, the letter carries no weight whatsoever?

The next day arrives, I'm weary from having no sleep at all due to the strain of the situation and coupled with this, later that day is the funeral of a close friend of mine who died young from a stomach ulcer. I was in complete turmoil. But what rides above this adversity, is a strong determination for what's right. Yes, it would be easier to plead guilty, take the charge and avoid the stress of the situation, but I battled on, to address this police officer's incompetence and unprofessional conduct.

I arrived at court again, produced all of my evidence and insurance documents and finally, I won. The case was dismissed.

I wondered if the police officer had heard how this case went. I thought back to him boastfully repeating "see you in court" to me. Yes I thought, you did see me in court – and I won.

But you have to think to yourself, what a waste of government time and money. Chasing a farcical conviction that no judge would uphold, all due to the mistakes made by the initial police officer. He clearly needs to be retrained on how to read and evaluate insurance policies. No wonder this country is in the state it is, when our patrons of the law can't even administer their powers or jurisdiction properly.

I am now entitled to a full refund of the compound penalty charge I paid to get the car back, but this was not about the money. What's pivotal to me is that I proved the police officer wrong, and I acted, I stood up for myself.

I understand that some police trainers advise new recruits in training that 'if they feel something is wrong, then it normally is'.

Well I feel this works both ways and when I felt something was not right with the police officer, I was right.

And this is far from an isolated case. A recent article in the national press highlighted the growing trend of rude police officers who have been told to stop 'speaking sarcastically' to the public. As many as 25% of complaints brought against the police were for rudeness, and subsequently many forces have opted to send officers on 'anti-rudeness' courses to improve their interaction skills.

But I haven't finished yet. For all of this unnecessary stress he put me through, I want answers. And most of all, I want to be sure he won't do this to someone else who is innocent.

*JJ*

## Mixed Relationships and Crossing Cultures

It's all about personal choice when choosing a partner; I personally have always had a preference for Jamaican men. It's more of a cultural thing, I suppose, everything that goes with it, the food, the music, their mannerisms, the talk, the walk, etc. – all of this attracts me. To be sexually attracted to someone boils down to who you are naturally attracted to, which in many ways is not determined by the colour of a person's skin. So who should really care if you choose a partner of a different race to your own? It's a wonderful experience, believe me, to share one another's culture.

Britain today is one of the greatest melting pots, with so many different races, religions, ethnicities, etc. The world is *our* oyster when it comes to choice, so it's inevitable that some of us will cross cultures when it comes to relationships and marriage. I can imagine that one day the whole of Britain will be mixed race. It's taken fifty years for Britain to 'mix' happily with other races.

I remember it being a lot less tolerant when I brought my Jamaican boyfriend home to meet my parents thirty years ago, to a predominantly 'white' village. I must admit we attracted some odd looks, but when people heard him sing and dance at our local pub they joined in and made him feel welcome. At the end of the day, it's up to you who you choose to share your life with, and if you decide to have a partner of a different race than your own, good luck to you and enjoy every minute of it! I know I did.

Having said that, I'd be more worried about the state this country is in than the skin tone of the person you lay down with at night. We just have to hope that this recession won't create an embittered and racist underclass. It could cause a minority of people who lose their jobs to look for targets, 'scapegoats' on whom to take out their bitterness and anger. I hope this dreadful recession will not last. But we must not let its legacy be a bitter and angry underclass.

*JJ*

## Love Music, Hate Racism

It's amazing to witness an array of different cultures in one place, and this is what I experienced at the "Love Music, Hate Racism" festival at Stoke-on-Trent. It was truly amazing!

I am deeply grateful to the *Daily Mirror* for raising awareness with its bus of "hope not hate", especially as my children are of mixed race origin.

I travelled from the valleys of South Wales to give my support. Thousands of people participated in enjoying music from many of today's stars including Kelly Rowland, Kano, Pete Doherty, The Beat, Mutya Buena, Roll Deep and many more.

The festival inspired me to become a member of "Join Unite Against Fascism", and I hope many more people will do so. We don't want the BNP to rule us, our country and cause social unrest and destruction between the people of Britain. We don't want a repeat of the 1980s.

We have come so far since the Stephen Lawrence murder which broke the hearts of so many. The BNP want to undo all the good in our society because they don't like diversity. They can never break that.

The BNP don't care about the people of Britain, they only care about themselves and their own views; they are evil, they "Love to Hate". If they had their way we would have no black doctors or nurses, no black footballers and no black musicians, and our culture wouldn't be as richly diverse as it is today.

There is no place in our society for these evil organisations, so don't allow them to fool you into voting for them through our vulnerability as our country struggles out of recession, because believe me, they will turn on you in the end.

Not only would I like to thank the *Daily Mirror* for organising the "Bus of Hope" campaign, I would also like to thank them for offering me support when I began my career in modelling. It was through the *Daily Mirror* that I was signed up by one of London's top modelling agencies. The advice and support given to me by a *Daily Mirror* employee, Penny Burton, when she saw my modelling pictures, allowed me to carve out my modelling career and fulfil my ambition at that time.

Peace and take care,

*JJ*

## BNP, Outrageous Remarks

I cannot believe that the Leader of the British Nationalist Party, Nick Griffin, made the outrageous statement that there is "no such thing as a black Welshman". What a load of rubbish!

I am Welsh through and through. My two children are of mixed race origin and were born in Wales, which makes them Welsh regardless of the colour of their skin, but we are also proud of their mixed Caribbean heritage too. They have the best of both worlds.

I bring my attention today to a well-loved and respected black Welshman, Vaughan Gething, who was the first black president of Wales TUC and a high-ranking and well-revered solicitor. I was particularly moved when I heard that Mr Gething had stated: "I know that I'm proud of who and what I am. I know this is my country – our country."

I have written about him in a previous column and also draw comparisons with Barack Obama himself.

If the BNP had their way, we wouldn't have had greats such as Gething, black footballers, black doctors, nurses and so on. We wouldn't have had Tiger Bay's own international superstar diva Shirley Bassey, or the world-beating, celebrated athlete Colin Jackson. They want us to believe their lies and brainwash the people of Britain, causing a breakdown in society.

I was in Birmingham on the 8th August when the BNP were protesting, and the amount of anti-racist groups that turned out to defend the people of Britain was astronomical. They should realise that wherever they go in Britain, they will be followed and fought against and that there is nowhere to hide in this nation.

They cannot and will not get away with what they are trying to do. We are a mixed race, multi-cultural Britain, and we are here to stay and flourish. So get used to it, Nick Griffin and the BNP.

I watched with vested interest and great anxiety the highly anticipated *Question Time* episode featuring Nick Griffin and I am happy at both the outcome and the way he conducted himself. Critically assessed as "bad for him and his party", I watched as he licked his lips nervously as he was pulled apart by the panel and audience.

His comments that "if Winston Churchill were alive today he would be a member of the BNP" were as ludicrous as the integrity of Nick Griffin himself. Churchill was one of, if not the greatest' leaders we have ever had. He would turn in his grave if he knew of this outrageous claim.

Churchill fought tooth and nail against the likes of Nick Griffin, fascists and the Nazi party, which is why he led us to war against Hitler and won in 1944. As I have previously stated, the Polish helped us and we helped them, and Churchill said the Polish would be welcome in Britain forever more.

Winston Churchill was everything the BNP are not, and never will be.

I cannot believe that after *Question Time*, because of his bad performance and lack of support, he tried to twist things, saying it was only because the programme was filmed in London. He challenged *Question Time* to "come up to the North" because "it's different up there", as if this was a pugilistic fight, not a democratic discussion.

Well I went up North, to Stoke-on-Trent, where Nick Griffin's constituency is, to the "Love Music – Hate Racism" event. Believe me, if Griffin had appeared here he wouldn't have stood a chance, because the amount of people who turned up in protest at his vile views would have outnumbered any support he could have ever gathered.

The only reason he gained seats and became an MEP is because our country is struggling out of recession. Nick Griffin is harnessing the feeling of despair and plight as we endeavour to bring the economy out of this slump, picking up on the negativity to further his ill-founded views and policies and try to gain support for them. He wants us to think he has changed; he hasn't, and he should realise he is fighting a useless cause, he will never win.

The BNP try to stir up hatred and violence, and we do not want to see a repeat of the 80s with riots across the country, undoing all the good work we have done since then. Just because they are trying to front a new suited image to the party, they hope the new image will prove beneficial in recruiting new supporters, lest we forget its hideous origins and face of the past.

So thank you to the BBC, and their freedom of speech ethos, which allowed millions of people across the UK to see firsthand what a slime-ball and racist bigot Nick Griffin truly is.

*JJ*

## Michael Jackson

I would like to pay tribute to the one and only Michael Jackson, who sadly passed away on 25th June 2009.

I always say that there is always someone better, it is an old saying my mother instilled in me as a child, but there will never be anyone better than Michael Jackson.

My heart goes out to his three beautiful children and his family. His children are in the best care possible, with his mother. They have aunties, uncles and cousins who love them dearly and with this level of support and love behind them, I am sure they will grow up to be fine people.

His daughter, Paris, did him proud at his funeral with her heart-breaking speech and showed the world just how normal and caring his children are. This proved there was nothing strange about her daddy, but what was strange was what he had to put up with from all the intrusiveness, the rumours, speculation and invasion of privacy.

I cannot help thinking that if his daughter had said these things whilst he was alive, then all the 'Wacko Jacko' nonsense which he hated would have ceased to exist; that we would have accepted him as a normal, loving father who was no different when it came to loving his children than you or I. But then, why should he have had to place his children on show in the world media's eye just to please others?

There is no doubt that he was looking down on Paris that sad day and would have been so very proud of his little girl.

It was also great to see our very own Shaheen Jafargholi from *Britain's Got Talent* who sang one of Michael's songs, "Who's loving you", at the funeral. Michael was impressed with this young star after seeing his performance on YouTube; no doubt he reminded him of himself as a young star.

Shaheen – who only lives twenty miles from me, and we are all very proud of him – paid his own tribute to Michael, saying he loved him and will miss him always.

Just as Minister Al Sharpton, a human rights activist, said to Michael's children, "Wasn't nothing strange about your Daddy. It was strange what your Daddy had to deal with. But he dealt with it anyway." To me, as a mother, that statement is all that Michael's children would have needed to hear. That was all that would have been needed to help them through their grief and to overcome the negativity that surrounded their father in the media. It is hard enough to deal with death alone, and even harder when you have to deal with what people are saying as well. That would be difficult for any child.

Michael Jackson may have been the King of Pop, but to me and many others he was the King of the World, bringing people of all races and cultures together. One of his ambitions was to walk on the moon, and no doubt he would have achieved that too. But that is what Michael did, he made you believe. I do not think I would have been surprised if he had walked on air; he was a genius who astounded and amazed people. Anything was possible with Michael.

No-one is immortal, but he will live on forever in our hearts and thoughts. He was gentle, loving, caring and generous. I could go on and on. What he did for Live Aid shone on like a star, helping the world. He was the world.

RIP Michael, no doubt you are looking down, maybe now you realise how much you were loved and always will be. God bless.

*JJ*

## King and Queen Beauty Competition

The stage was set, ten beautiful black women and one man were the finalists of a beauty competition held in Birmingham last August, organised by Ms Mac and S & G Graphix. As the finalists were whittled down, it became more and more difficult to select the winners. After long debate and discussion, the two winners were chosen. I must say it was easier to select the male winner as there was only one contestant "Mr Mac" who was the only man brave enough to compete.

I was honoured to represent *The Big Eye* as a judge for the competition, and the winners received many wonderful gifts including aftershaves/perfumes and stunning clothes from swimwear and lingerie to gorgeous evening gowns.

The 'after party' was held at the Function Suite on Moseley Road. The atmosphere as we entered the club was ecstatic. There was a strong Jamaican theme throughout the club. The food they put on included all the Jamaican favourites such as jerk chicken, curry goat, rice 'n' peas, etc. The live singers were amazing; one sounded like Gregory Isaacs and the other like Sanchez, I'm not joking. We partied the night away!

When I arrived back in Wales, all that partying reminded me of the times I had in Kingston, Jamaica, at the Turntable Club; it brought back so many memories. I was always the last one out of the club. I remember the times we had in London, going back twenty years, and notice how things have changed. There are fewer blues 'illegal house parties'. I asked a few people why this is and they informed me that the police had stopped them.

I remember in my day going to "Chicken Blues" in East London, where we would stroll out of there at eight in the morning, seeing people standing by the bus stop on their way to work, staring up at us in awe. I remember my friends would refuse to come along with me most of the time, but it was where I wanted to be. I loved the atmosphere, the Reggae music, the curry goat that they served on white paper plates: everything about it was exciting. The times my friends refused to go with me, I decided to go alone. I used to go to a club in Dalston, North London, called the "4 Aces". I would arrive at the club around three or four in the morning, as that was the time it started to fill. Sometimes I felt embarrassed on my own, so if anyone asked me who I was waiting for I would pretend I was waiting for a friend, although that friend would never turn up, and they didn't need to for me to enjoy myself. Nevertheless, the people there were always friendly, that is what Jamaican people are like, and they welcome you with open arms. Even at the end of the night, or rather in the early morning, I would always ask the taxi driver to wait until I put the key in my door, just to make sure I was home safely. You could say I lived dangerously, but then in other ways I always tried to be careful.

I have seen people change their lifestyle many times, but I can honestly say that I will never change the way I feel about the Caribbean culture I have embraced over the decades. I may live in a modestly quiet part of the country but it will never stop me enjoying the music, the food, etc. I have created my own cultural world and taught my two children, who are of Caribbean descent, the values of the culture, and I am glad I have lived it, or my children wouldn't have had the heavy Jamaican influence they have had. I have taught them both sides of their culture, enabling them to have the best of both worlds, which I think mixed race children are blessed to have.

The competition had been a mixture of nerves and excitement for me, a truly amazing experience and one I look back on with utmost pride. But looking back, I shriek with horror thinking how tense and thrown I was by the last minute change the organisers landed on me. I was to host the competition instead of being just one of the judges. As you can imagine, a last moment revelation like this totally impaled a sense of anxiety on me, took me out of the comfort zone I'd prepared myself to be in and pushed me completely in the limelight, talk about thrown in at the deep end!

But this sense of shock and horror was pale in comparison compared to what was about to unfold unbeknownst to us all later on...

Even now when I watch the DVD, I still recoil in shock at the moment the runner up in the competition attacked the winner. She jumped on her to fight in what was reminiscent of a boxing ring contest, not a beauty one as it was fully intended. You could see her face filled with pure rage and overwhelming emotion, barely able to contain her anger at not winning until this urge took over and she lashed out.

I still remember vividly how my reactions to what was unfolding panned out. My brain immediately signalled me to protect myself, to stand back and not get involved in the melee, simply to wait for the security guards that surely would come storming in any second to resolve the fight. After all, nobody else around me was getting involved, this was the sensible thing to do.

But there was no sign of security. Seconds passed in what felt like hours, why was this being allowed to continue, where was the help? I could feel myself perspiring, my brain a flurry of activity and a sense of fear. It was then this flurry of emotion that brought myself to spontaneous action, I had to do something. If I didn't, who knows what could happen, how bad this could escalate and quickly.

Heart first, head following, I jumped between the two contestants in a bid to separate them. I had to use every ounce of my strength to physically part the women, as if to form a human protective barrier. I knew I not only had to intervene physically, but also had to try and reason with them as otherwise they would have continued to grasp and claw at each other, driven by hatred.

I tried to explain how they are both beautiful, they'd both done extremely well in the competition but, like every competition, there can only be one winner. This seemed to work, and when the adrenaline slowed down, they made up as friends. It was at that moment that security turned up, 'impeccable timing' I thought. They even jokingly offered me a job in security.

I felt proud that I chose to stand up and break up the fight, resolving it peacefully when others around me took a step back. Who knows what could have happened, it's a safe bet serious injury was the least to be expected when two women go at each other with intent to hurt one another badly.

I was very nervous hosting this competition. I know a beauty contest isn't on the same scale as something like the X-factor, but to me it was MY Ex-Factor, something that although on a smaller scale, filled me with pride to be asked to play the role of judge, and then the role of host. And oh yes, also the role of security! It's something I will never forget. And somehow I don't think you'd ever see Simon Cowell jumping on stage to separate two fighting contestants!

*JJ*

## Separation and Divorce

This month I would like to highlight the point that children can have a better upbringing in a single-parent household than being brought up with two parents who argue. A household which argues all the time can be very damaging to the children. I can relate to this due to my own circumstances. I have been a single mother for many years and have brought up my two children alone. One is currently at university and the other is a successful cricketer. I am very proud of my children, and I am beginning to feel proud of myself for nurturing and encouraging them. I believe that if I didn't have the courage to get a divorce and realise things were not right for my children then their future may well be very different.

I have to admit I am saddened by the Katie Price and Peter Andre separation. Katie Price seems to be getting all the blame for the break-up, especially when it seemed Peter Andre left her. It doesn't seem fair that Katie has received the majority of the criticism for the separation, but what people do not realise is that this woman has been through a lot in her life and I know there are many others like her too. My advice to her would be to keep strong and not to worry too much about what people gossip about you. I understand it's easier said than done, and believe me, I've been there and I know you can rise above it and follow your dreams.

I can't recall one article which has 'stuck up' for Katie Price but I would like to stress I am supporting her as I can see both sides of the situation, not just one. It seems as though because Katie Price is so outspoken, she is receiving all the blame. The criticism Katie is receiving also highlights the fact that many people are jealous of what she has achieved in her life. To be able to forge a successful career out of her beauty takes real talent, and people who dislike her for whatever reason display signs of jealousy.

All of the controversy surrounding the couple, I believe, has overshadowed the real importance of the break-up, and that is the future of the young children they have together. My advice to both of them and to other people in their situation is to try to be sensible and friendly for the children's sake. I soon learned to do this after my divorce with my children's father. It does get better in time; the only ones to get hurt through all of this are the children. Going through my divorce I hated my children's father, but we are now good friends.

I only wish that the divorce wasn't so volatile at the beginning, as my one child remembers it and she went through a hard time for a while.

In 1986 I began a career in modelling, and I have been working in the beauty industry. I remember seeing 'Jordan' modelling in a newspaper column and told my friend that she was going to be a successful model. My friend disagreed at the time, and I'm glad to say I proved her wrong, as Jordan became one of the most famous models of all time.

I am confident of one thing, that I can spot beauty when I see it, and felt honoured to host a beauty competition in Birmingham in August. I am aware that there is a lot of jealousy surrounding Jordan, but she has managed to rise above it and turn her beauty into mega stardom as she made the transition into perfume, books and clothing. To all the people who slate her, I think it's time to realise that we need to get used to her, because she is in our lives for a long time to come.

I think that she has one of the most beautiful faces in the world. I hope things work out for the sake of the children, and I'm sure they will.

*JJ*

## Madonna's Mixed Race Family

As you know, I feel very passionate about our mixed race population and feel that it is important for a child of mixed race heritage, or a child growing up in a mixed race family, to learn and *not* be allowed to forget their heritage and cultural needs. This is why I am taking a great interest in Madonna's adoption of little Mercy James, whom she adopted in June 2009, and I am very happy to hear that she wants little Mercy to learn all about her culture and the place where she was born.

My message to Madonna is, you are doing the right thing. It will save the heartache of when she's older. Instead of having to search for her roots she will grow with them, which is a wonderful thing. I count myself lucky as my two children are of mixed race origin and I have lived both cultures, so for me it came easy.

Madonna found herself in a heart-breaking situation when at one point she was told she couldn't adopt the little girl after they had bonded. Can you imagine how they both felt to be torn apart? She was determined to fight her case when Judge Esme Chombo said that Madonna was ineligible to adopt Mercy as she didn't qualify as a Malawian resident, but through her determination and love for Mercy, she is now the girl's proud mother.

At the time, the judge made it clear that she didn't want to make it easy for child trafficking, and I am glad she made this statement. Although Madonna herself found it a heart-breaking time, I bet she is happy with this statement, because the last thing we want is for child trafficking to go on in Africa or anywhere in the world. On the contrary, Madonna is in the limelight and her children will also grow up in it, which means we will all watch them grow as a family.

I think that she is a wonderful person for taking two children out of poverty, and she will give them a good life with a one-to-one mother's love. Taking them from an African orphanage, it wasn't made easy for her because of who she is. It is also very sad that she is separated from her husband, Guy Richie. He is still a loving father, and she is the proud mother of her two adopted children, Mercy James and David Banda, and her biological children, Lourdes and Rocco. She is now a single parent, like me. It can be hard sometimes, but also very rewarding and positive. It can also make you more determined to encourage your children to strive and do well in life. I know I have!

Madonna has done a great deal for charity over the years, and is currently helping to fund a school in Africa. I wish her and her family all the love, joy and happiness always, and the one beautiful gift she can give them is the best of both worlds.

God bless.

*JJ*

## Cage Fighting, Bringing Us Together

Hi readers.

Cage fighting seems to be the buzz word at the moment and it has become part of the sporting agenda on our TV sets. Even our very own beautiful Katie Price has begun dating a well-known cage fighter, Alex Reid.

Cage fighting sounds a scary concept, but the reality is that it's a professional sport under the heading of mixed martial arts and it is not as violent as some people make it out to be. It has rules just like any other sport such as wrestling, boxing and rugby.

Tensions were high, and the excitement in the air was just extraordinary as I stepped into a local leisure centre to watch an evening of cage fighting. An array of fighters from all different cultural backgrounds came to compete, including our very own Ryan "Ditto" Williams, twenty-three, who fights out of Active Bodies MMA. His opponent was Scott Sawyer, nineteen, fighting out of D Tech gym Birmingham.

Scott Sawyer won the bout after a very difficult judge's decision, because Ryan Williams fought so well and only lost on points. It was miraculous to watch as both opponents put on an excellent fight, and I can honestly say I have never seen anything like it. It got the adrenaline flowing, so I can only imagine what the fighters were going through.

Ryan Williams gave 110% and I am personally a fan of his now.

It was so pleasing to see the array of different people from different cultural backgrounds from all over the country enjoying the evening, and it was great to get the fighters to model *The Big Eye* newspaper in a photograph.

I believe Ryan is an aspiration for all of us who want to achieve things in life, and the only way to do so is through hard work, dedication, confidence and never giving up.

After watching the extraordinary events of that exciting September evening I couldn't stop thinking how important it is to be able to have the skills to defend yourself. One particularly scary memory come to mind when I was younger living in London. My ex-Jamaican boyfriend at the time was a martial arts expert in Kung Fu. He also taught it in his spare time.

His experience saved his life one night out in the West End of London when another man came at him with a machete in a Shebeen (an illegal house party). The man cornered my ex like a rat and violently swung for him. My ex used his martial arts to block every blow of the machete. It was a truly terrifying ordeal. He came out of that Shebeen without a mark on his body. He defended himself the correct way and no one was hurt.

The following night, in some bizarre fashion, the same attacker came over and shook my ex-boyfriend's hand and that was that!

I understand Kung Fu is different from cage fighting in some respects, but they are both effective ways of defending yourself, as was the case with my ex-boyfriend, and also outside a nightclub in Swansea, South Wales, in September this year when two cage fighters dressed up as women for fun on a night out were picked on by two yobs. They tried to pick a fight with them, not realising they were cage fighters and how powerful their punches were. They had their comeuppance, that's for sure!

*JJ*

## Slumdog Millionaire "Spot On"

Some time ago I paid tribute to a businessman and friend, Alan Jones, aka "Bronco", who sadly passed away in January 2009. He was a young fifty-five-year-old who mixed with all cultures. I explained in my tribute that he loved to travel, and his real love was India.

Christmas day 2009, his beloved wife and two sons decided to follow on in his footsteps and take a trip to India, which Bronco visited every year, sometimes for months on end. His dream was for his ashes to be scattered across the Indian Ocean.

They combined this pilgrimage for their late husband and father with a holiday to enjoy India, as Bronco would not have wanted them to visit this country he held so dear on only heartbreaking terms.

They were joined on the trip by a host of close friends, including my son James, as he looked upon Bronco as a father figure and had great respect for the man. My son explained that scattering the ashes was an incredibly emotional time, but he would have been so proud. No doubt Bronco was looking down on them all that day.

The group began their journey Christmas night and flew from Heathrow to Mumbai, which is regarded by many as the new Bombay. They stayed for two nights and then began a twelve-hour journey by train.

The trains aren't anything like the British trains we're accustomed to. They're crammed with people begging, some selling whatever they can get their hands on just to be able to eat. Disabled people, some blind, some without limbs, dragging themselves through the aisles of the speeding, incredibly hot trains. So disabled, yet so independent.

But what stood out about this journey, explained my son, was that the people were so very friendly to them all; it certainly was an eye-opener for him. He told of how the toilet had no doors, and metal bars instead of windows. It certainly puts into perspective how fortunate we are and would make us think twice about complaining about a short delay on one of our trains.

The train finally arrived at its destination; the whole group gets off, all sticking together. They shout along the line to remind everyone to get their possessions before the train leaves. My son suddenly realises he has left his rucksack on the train. Panicking, he shouts, "My bag!", and someone shouts back for him to just leave it. Then he realised his passport was in it. Now the panic really set in, as he realised he was not going to be able to get home without it The group watch in total horror as my son jumps on the now moving train to get his bag.

Fortunately, the train didn't have doors, so he had a chance to jump on before it moved away. As the train picked up momentum, he knew he had to act fast. It's lucky my son is an accomplished sportsman, as I shudder to think what could have happened had he not been as nimble or as agile as he is. He sprinted beside the train and managed to jump aboard. Frantically scuffling through the carriages screaming "My bag!" and pointing to it above the seats, the nearby passengers grabbed it and passed it to him.

He then ran to the exit, grasped the bag tightly to his chest, as if to offer protection, a padded landing as it were, took a deep breath and leapt from the train.

James landed abruptly, and dust flew up as he rolled down the bank. The crowd that was gathered could not believe what they had witnessed, and comforted him as he physically shook from the impact and the adrenalin. I'm sure it was the adrenalin that had made this possible and I thank God he is still alive to tell this tale.

My son was meant to stay for three weeks but decided to come home after one. He simply wasn't prepared for all the poverty and suffering he saw. It certainly is an eye-opener for a young man who is used to living in comparative luxury in this country compared to many parts of India.

On a similar note, my nephew Nicholas, who went to work in Manila in the Philippines for his company for several months in 2008, had first-hand experience of real poverty and desperation that saw children as young as three years old begging on busy roads as cars stopped at lights. This was an eye-opener to him, like my son in India, as children in the UK don't see a life like this growing up.

Despite finding it hard to cope with seeing such poverty, James is adamant his lasting memory of the trip was how friendly the people were, this exemplified by them helping him with his bag on the train.

When he arrived home, we watched the film *Slumdog Millionaire* together. He showed me pictures of the train he travelled on, which was identical to that in the film, and how the film depicts exactly how life is in Mumbai, with children begging but at the same time always happy regardless of their situation.

I'm glad my son went on this trip and shared the experience that he did. While many of his friends of the same age spent their holidays last year in places like Ibiza and Magaluf, he was somewhere where he could experience and immerse himself in real culture. I know the whole trip had made him realise how fortunate he is and how worse off some countries really are.

One of the bars they visited blasted out Reggae music and the locals were happy to pose for photos with *The Big Eye* newspaper and the Jamaican t-shirt.

*Slumdog Millionaire* is available to buy now on DVD.

## *JJ*

## Channel Four's Slum Secret Millionaire

After writing the column on '*Slumdog Millionaire* – Spot On', I watched with great interest in January this year Channel Four's *Slumdog Secret Millionaire*. This was about a wealthy business entrepreneur, Sheema Sharma, who visits and experiences life in the Mumbai slums.

Her mission was to help the people there as much as she can, whilst integrating herself within them and not letting on that she is a wealthy businesswoman. The premise is that of *Secret Millionaire* shown in this country. After spending time in the slums, Sheema's intention was to make a generous donation to help change the lives of people she encountered on her journey.

It was heart-breaking for her, and also for me, watching the programme, to witness children as young as five years old, working on dumping grounds going through thousands of tons of garbage to earn a few rupees just so they can afford to eat.

The massive divide between rich and poor is no more evident than in India. Many families live on pavements or underneath structures just to get shade from the sun. The people of India feel it's important for the world to see this gulf in wealth and privilege and witness it through documentaries like this one.

One little boy, aged just eight, was forced to work the streets collecting cardboard for recycling so he could support his mother and sister after his father's death. Nobody made him do this, but when questioned why he was doing it, he simply replied, "Who else would feed my family?" Yet still, these children are so friendly and polite, despite their social deprivation, because it's the only way they know to be.

A local lady gave up her job to set up a project called 'Sweata', a toy bank where she collected toys and distributed them to local children and orphanages. Another lady ran a 'school on wheels', a bus of hope, which travelled to very poor areas and picked up children who wouldn't have any other chance of an education. When the children saw the bus coming, they would run to it enthusiastically, shouting and waving, such a warming sight that brought tears running down my face. They called it the Door Step School.

The day before Sheema's departure, she had to decide whom she was going to donate her money to. It was, of course, a very difficult decision to make, as everyone she had encountered was so very deserving. Sheema decided to donate to the Door Step School, the toy bank, a family that lived on the pavement and the eight-year-old boy who was supporting his family; she paid for him to go to school for ten years.

I watched in awe at Sheema's face of pure delight and the pleasure she gained from helping these worthy people and, in turn, the sheer gratefulness in those receiving. I couldn't help thinking that being generous is a gift from God.

It brought back memories of when I visited a children's home in London many years ago. I took a box of crisps and some chocolate for them to share, and of how much more pleasure I gain from giving rather than receiving. I only wish I was in a better position to make a big difference. But lest we forget, it doesn't matter how much you give or how small a donation to charity, it all helps and that could be our way of making a difference.

I mentioned in my earlier article about my nephew, Nicholas, living and working in Manila in the Philippines in 2008. Christmas in the Philippines is massive. They start celebrating in September and it goes on well into the New Year. Wanting to give something back to this place they'd been calling home for many months, they visited a home for abandoned physically and mentally disabled children called "The Chosen Children Village" and decided to dress as Santa and take as many gifts as they could gather beforehand. It was a remarkable visit, and they felt so good to bring happiness to these very special children, especially little Nino, who was born without arms and legs, and now, aged just three, smiled broadly at them as they distributed the presents. If ever there was a reality check of how fortunate we are, and how we should use this fortune to benefit those worse off wherever and whenever we can, then that was it.

There is an organisation called Action Aid, where you can sponsor a child for as little as 50p a day. I know not everyone can commit to this continuously, but even a one-off gesture goes a long way to making a difference.

I'm glad there are programmes like *Slumdog Secret Millionaire*, as without the medium of television, we wouldn't be aware of these global issues and how we can help. I know it made me feel both very lucky and extremely humbled.

*JJ*

# Black Models

In this column, I will be discussing the need for more black, mixed race and Asian models to appear in our advertising campaigns, on the cover of our glossy magazines, in films, TV and all aspects of the media. Our country is an ever growing 'melting pot' and we need to make sure the balance is just.

We need more role models. People like Naomi Campbell, Tyra Banks and the beautiful Iman, who is married to David Bowie. She was the first black woman to grace the covers of the major glossy magazines, such as *Vogue*, and shot to stardom within months of first being noticed. The Somalia-born beauty is as stunning as ever today in her mid-fifties, and was a muse for many designers including Yves Saint-Laurent, who famously said, "My dream woman is Iman."

Back in my day as a young model it was rare to see black mannequins in shop windows, or mixed race marriages in soaps or films. One of the only programmes to display this was *Love Thy Neighbour*, which was negative. I'm glad things have changed, as it shows how much we have come on as a nation. Britain now has one of the highest rates of inter-racial relationships in the western world, with one in ten children growing up in a mixed ethnicity home, and it's good to see real life and the way the country actually stands portrayed in the programmes we watch.

Mixed race people are projected to be the largest minority group by the year 2025. They are already contributing to our society more than any other group, so I'm not surprised things are changing in a big way. Of course, these statistics are of particular interest to me as a mother of two mixed race children.

I think modelling agencies should reflect on ethnic diversity. When I started modelling in the late 1970s and 1980s we had our own black page three girl, Gillian De Turville. We used to party together at the nightclub 'Main Squeeze' on the Kings Road, London, and Gillian was one of the nicest people I have ever met. Gillian went on to appear in the world-famous Pirelli calendar in 1987, which puts her alongside such modelling giants as Naomi Campbell, Heidi Klum and Gisele Bundchen.

I took a great interest in the June 2008 issue of Italian *Vogue* magazine when its editor, Franca Sozzani, made the decision to only feature black models in that particular edition. The pictures were taken by Steven Meisel, who is based in New York and is one of the most successful photographers in the industry.

Many big names in the fashion world would have formed a protest in New York to highlight the problems faced by black models. They explained in a letter to the *Guardian* newspaper on 20th June 2008 that the absence of black models on the covers of fashion magazines has long been a complaint within the industry. Steven Meisel himself is quoted as saying: "Perhaps the designers, perhaps the magazine editors. They are the powerful people. And the advertisers. I have asked my advertising clients so many times, 'Can we use a black girl?' They say no. Their concern is that consumers will resist the product. It all comes down to money."

Franca Sozzani explained that her decision was influenced by the New York group as well as by Barack Obama's success in the US presidential primaries.

I'm pleased she was impressed but find it sad that it had to be influenced by the soon-to-be President and not the true sense of the problem, and the great wealth of talent and beauty of our black and mixed race models.

You can go online and view a modelling agency that specialises in diversity at www.urbanangelsagency.com.

*JJ*

## "Saluting our Unsung Heroines" – 100 years of International Woman's Day

I was extremely surprised and ecstatically happy in March 2010 when I received a call from the *Daily Mirror* explaining that my daughter had nominated me for the "Woman of the Year" award. The award was celebrating 100 years of International Woman's Day and my daughter praised me for always being there for her and her brother James, and how we got through a divorce from her father when both children were very young.

We went through a hard time, but I reassured them that everything was going to be fine and we'd get through it, together. I told them that just because they're from a broken family home this had no bearing on them and did not mean they were any less special than anyone else.

I feel strongly about education, and placed a great deal of emphasis on the fact that it is the key to a successful and prosperous life and future. My own parents didn't share these views on the importance of education, and as a result didn't encourage me at school.

I was determined to do everything within my power to ensure that my children had the opportunities that I didn't have growing up. I played both a mum and dad role during their childhood to make their home life as happy and as normal as possible. It's especially important, I feel, for the son to have a father figure around, and I made every effort possible to encourage my son, James, in all sports. I would drive him to all of his practices, sessions and matches, and made sure he had everything he needed to compete. He has now grown up to be an extremely talented athlete and competitor, playing rugby amongst other sports, and is always being cited in the newspapers for his success as a cricketer.

The 100 years of International Woman's Day special *Daily Mirror* supplement was edited by the Prime Minister's wife, Sarah Brown. She explains in the edition how things have changed over the past 100 years for women and how they now hold an equal footing to their male counterparts. Women can apply for any job, vote, and have access to free healthcare, all of which were unheard of 100 years ago. She goes on to say how much of the progress made over this time can be accredited to the courage and determination of those before us such as Florence Nightingale, Marie Curie and the Pankhurst family. They have truly paved the way for those of us today who enjoy greater freedom, equality and independence.

Joan Bakewell, the TV presenter, government ageism tsar and writer, also explains in this edition how things have changed over the years. How in Victorian days childbirth was a considerable danger to women. I can relate to this on a personal level as my grandmother died giving birth, leaving my father and his brothers and sisters without a mother, forcing the eldest sister to take on the motherly role and raise the children.

Now we have the best free healthcare system we could wish for, with doctors and nurses from all over the globe integrating with our own doctors and nurses here, not forgetting the special maternity units built within our hospitals as well. Healthcare today is easily taken for granted, but it's worth reflecting on what our great-grandparents and grandparents had when they were growing up.

I feel extremely honoured and humbled by appearing in this special edition of the *Daily Mirror* and to be praised by Sarah Brown as an unsung hero along with three other winners. Yes, I am a 'winner' in so many senses, not least being a winner to my family, but being a winner for having the love of my family. I thank my daughter so much for nominating me for the award, and it should be known it wasn't won for me, but for every single parent out there. I hope they can be inspired by my story and how I struggled as a single parent. Encourage your children always, in everything they do. Help nurture them and put education at the forefront of your focus for them. I'm so very proud that despite the adversity, and despite the hurdles we had in front of us as a single-mother family, my son and daughter are prospering in this world, and if I could do it alone, anyone can.

When my daughter Jilly was accepted into university to study computer science, it meant that all those years of hard work and toil were finally paying off. I'm so very proud of her, and James too, who's studying for an NVQ in business right now. My children's accomplishments are a huge source of joy to me, a feeling of sheer gratification that makes me glow inside.

Being nominated is an honour that will stick with me forever. In the days spent bringing my two wonderful children up alone and fighting to make sure they had every advantage I could give them, I never dreamt in a million years that one day I would be invited to Number 10 Downing Street for tea. It's something that I'll cherish for the rest of my days and something I can proudly recount to my children's children, as hopefully they will embrace parenthood in the future as well.

*JJ*

## Tea at No. 10 – March 2010

This is a follow-up column to me being invited to Number 10 Downing Street for tea with the Prime Minister's wife, Sarah Brown. For me and the three other winners of the *Daily Mirror*'s 'Woman of the Year' contest, this was a treat from Sarah herself.

As previously mentioned, the nomination for this contest came from my daughter Jilly, as, she says, she wanted to give something back to me. It was very hard for both her and her brother James when her father and I divorced. They were both very young, but they remember it well. But we battled through it, together, as a single-parent family, and the just reward was this special visit to Downing Street, a trip which will stay in our memories forever.

The big day arrived. The *Daily Mirror* had sent us our train tickets and we were met at Paddington Station by a chauffeur and whisked to Parliament Street, where we met up at a pub called The Red Lion which was oozing atmosphere. We were greeted there by Beth Neil from the *Mirror* and relaxed with food and drinks whilst awaiting the other guests of the day.

It was extremely exciting, everyone made a big effort and I must say we certainly all looked the part for such an occasion. It was also a pleasure to see all of the children who came with their mums on such good behaviour, and very well-mannered.

When everyone had arrived, we made our way across the road to Downing Street. After we had navigated the huge cast-iron black gates at the entrance we were, of course, subjected to strict security checks. After all, one of the most powerful men in the world resided here, and not just anyone can wander up to his less-than-humble abode!

And then there it was, Number 10! Synonymous as being the home of British politics and its leader's home and office, a truly enigmatic sight and one which sends shivers down your spine due to its rich tapestry of history. And there were my daughter and I, knocking on Number 10 to visit the Prime Minister's wife.

I thought to myself how this was a once-in-a-lifetime opportunity and how I was filled with immense pride, but my mind also took me back to how I had got here.

How many years ago my marriage broke down and I made the decision to leave Wales and seek a new life in London with my two small children. I remember how hard it was with no friends or relatives in this new 'world' for us as a family, no one to support us when the going got tough.

The children were not at nursery yet, but I found us a small place to live and I found myself trying as best I could to keep my children entertained and involved. We would go sightseeing, so as not to be stuck indoors all the time in such a restricted environment.

My young niece came up to visit us one day, so I put the children in a double-buggy and off we went to Parliament Street. And, fifteen years previous to this latest visit, we found ourselves by the

66

gates of Downing Street alongside many other tourists. To my utter astonishment, the police signalled towards us and asked if we would like to come up to Number 10 and have a tour. I thought he was joking at first, either that or he felt sorry for us, but it was a genuine offer.

As we approached the big black door with the small but poignant Number 10 sign on it I immediately recognised from watching the *News at Ten*, the little grey-haired man who used to poke his head around the door before he let you in, this was all so surreal.

I remember it was a Saturday and the Prime Minister at the time, John Major, wasn't at home. We were shown around but were told we were not allowed beyond a certain point for security reasons. On our second visit, in 2010, security seemed a lot tighter than in 1995 and I don't think this fortuitous occurrence would have been allowed today. I'm grateful technology has come on so much, and whereas my only souvenir of the 1995 visit is a Polaroid snap at the front door, 2010's visit was captured on digital camera. The photo of my daughter and I outside Number 10 is one I will treasure forever.

Living in London didn't last; I simply couldn't cope. I had made arrangements to stay, and had lined up a school for my daughter at Westminster, but we decided to head back home to Wales.

A memory that sticks involves my son James whilst in nursery back home in Wales being taught about 10 Downing Street. The teacher asked the class a question about it and my son raised his little hand eagerly ready to answer. He told the teacher he had been there, but the teacher did not give him a chance and accused him in front of the class of "telling porkies".

My son told me this, dejected, when he came home from school, so the very next day I went to the school, with the picture of us outside Number 10, to confront the teacher. The look on her face was priceless. In that moment it seemed that this teacher had made the assumption that James, one of two children of a single-parent Welsh valleys family, would never have got the chance to visit the home of the country's Prime Minister, only for it to be true, and made her question her rashness of judgement.

As I walked out, she blurted out, "May I ask why James was at Number 10?" But I walked on without giving her the satisfaction of a reply. She must have racked her brains, wondering how it could have come about. Was it a reward? Was it a prize? Was it due to an invite? And I laughed to myself that it was merely due to a kind gesture of a police officer. But that was then, and this time around it was due to achievement, and not chance.

We had a chat over tea with Sarah Brown. The rest of the group were the *Daily Mirror* representatives and the three other winners, one of whom was Mandi Boyle, who was devastated when her daughter Mollie, now just seven years of age, was diagnosed with Wilms' tumour, a kind of kidney cancer. Then there was Sheila Sapsed, who was nominated by friends because of her kindness in helping others, and Faiza Zaman, who is a team leader at a women's refuge that helps women and their children escape domestic violence.

We all got along really well and had in common this sense of disbelief of where we were right now. After tea we had a tour of this magnificent building, and history came to life with photos of ex-Prime Ministers like Harold Wilson, Margaret Thatcher and Winston Churchill. Each room was exquisite, and we were even shown the Cabinet Room, the very room in which wars had been declared. It was fascinating and very thought-provoking.

One room in particular interested me, one which had been decorated to Margaret Thatcher's taste, and slight markings were visible of where a bomb had hit it in the 1970s. Although it had many times since been touched-up, this marking remained, as if to leave a memory of the bomb and of the history. It was amazing to witness.

Sarah Brown was such a lovely lady, very calm and collected and with a definite aura around her. We discussed education together, an area we both stress the utmost importance of in this country and our children's development. She praised me for encouraging my children which resulted in my son and daughter both achieving academically, and how I did this alone as a single parent.

The Labour government place a massive emphasis on education, and it was nice to speak to someone who shared the same views and ideals. As I touched on in my last column, many parents don't place the same value on education, and this may be due to the fact that years ago it was only the well-off that went to university. This has changed radically now though, and there are opportunities out there for anyone who has the aim, desire and will to further themselves, and this comes from nurturing your children and encouraging them all the way, like I did with mine.

The Labour government has also put in place initiatives like school breakfast clubs so that every child has the chance to start the day right, enhancing their concentration and preparing them well for the day ahead. This has also made it a lot easier for any single parent, and also married couples, to go to work, knowing their children are being well catered for. They have also put in place resources for children struggling in school to receive the help needed to overcome any barriers and achieve their true potential.

Sarah also discussed the Gingerbread charity with me, explaining how it was set up to help single parents. I told her I would like to get involved and help in any way I could. I have since made some enquiries and an information pack is in the post.

I have tried to adequately verbalise it here, but no words can truly encapsulate my visit to Number 10, it was simply too special to describe. Thank you once again to my darling daughter for nominating me in the Woman of the Year Awards.

I would like to thank the *Daily Mirror* for looking after us so well on the day, and Sarah Brown, for her amazing hospitality and kindness.

*JJ*

# Election 2010
## Thursday 6th May 2010

Today is an exciting day for me. My children have reached voting age and are ready to vote for the first time. I feel very proud walking into the polling station with my daughter, ready to cast her first vote. I know one thing for sure, she will never forget the first time she voted, not only for this very reason but at one of the most exciting elections in history. With a hung parliament predicted, she couldn't wait to post on Facebook that she had voted, which I think is a good thing as it encourages younger voters, with more young people interested in politics than ever before exchanging their views and giving their own predictions. Also, I do think the televised ministerial debates have encouraged younger people to become more interested in politics. It is not quite midnight and I, like thousands of people across Britain, am eagerly awaiting the results of the election. I personally hope that our Prime Minister will still be Prime Minister on Friday 7th May. I have been watching the month-long campaign trail and remember the first day Gordon and Sarah Brown boarded a train at St Pancras Station, London, ready to start their campaign, and how Sarah supported her husband through thick and thin. I thought to myself what a wonderful thing, my vote and my heart is with Labour's Gordon Brown. I and thousands of others have no doubt that he is the man to run our country. I am watching this election on the *BBC News Election 2010*. I have just heard that Labour holds Llanelli, Wales's seat, and I am ecstatic at this point, as my father was born and bred in Llanelli before leaving to join the army. I am listening to Gordon Brown giving his speech in Scotland after winning 29,559 seats in Kirkcaldy and Cowenbeath. He goes on to say nearby is where he grew up and where his father preached. It's here, he says, that he learned what true friendship is. I have tears in my eyes listening to this speech. He thanked his wife, Sarah, for her love and support and also said he wouldn't let his people down.

They are still predicting a hung parliament, the first since 1974. Being Welsh myself, I am happy to see that Labour is doing well in Wales. Hundreds of voters have been unable to vote due to being turned away from the polling stations, which said they couldn't cope with the number of people turning up to vote. These people must be absolutely gutted and I sympathise with them. I am so glad that my family and I had the chance to vote. Impatiently waiting as the votes keep coming in, it has just been announced that Labour holds Merthyr Tydfil and Rhymney Gwent. "YES!" My fist is punched in the air at this victorious point, as Merthyr Tydfil is where I grew up.

## Friday 7th May 2010

It is 7.18 am. I have woken to the news that Gordon Brown is still the Prime Minister. The predictions were right and we now have a hung parliament. Despite the uncertainty, he is still Prime Minister. I believe he is on a rollercoaster at the moment and I hope that he will get off smoothly. It has been the most exciting election night for decades, with us all across Britain awaking to a hung parliament. This is similar to what happened in 1974 when the Prime Minister, Ted Heath (Conservative Prime Minister) resigned to Harold Wilson (Labour) becoming our Prime Minister. It is said that Ted Heath brooded over his decision for many years after; this is why I don't think that Gordon Brown should resign at this point without putting up the fight of his life for what he believes in, and I am sure he won't, then he won't be tormented by the 'what-ifs' and 'if-onlys'. If he decides to resign at the end of his fight, he can always be content that he, indeed, did not go without a fight and gave it his best shot, which I know he will. I know there are people saying that Gordon Brown isn't an elected Prime Minister, that he inherited it, but he is still our Prime Minister and this shouldn't be scorned upon. On the contrary, it should be looked up to. After all, he took on his predecessor's unfinished business and did his best, bringing us out of recession slowly but surely.

## *Sunday 9th May 2010*

It is now Sunday 9th May and MP Nick Clegg, Liberal Democrats, has been in talks with MP David Cameron, Conservatives, trying to strike a deal between them. It's like the ball is in Nick Clegg's court. He has to decide because of a hung parliament who he is going to side with, Labour or Conservative; I understand that he is in talks with Gordon Brown later on today. I must say it must be agonising for Nick Clegg but he has to put our country before his own preference. After all, he is the one who could make David Cameron Prime Minister. I personally can't see Nick Clegg siding with David Cameron, wanting to give tax cuts to the very rich, which is on the Conservative manifesto. A friend of mine told me that he changed his mind at the last minute and went from voting Labour to Lib Dem. He said if he thought for one minute that Nick Clegg was going to help make David Cameron Prime Minister he would have stuck with Labour. He said he didn't vote Lib Dems to get Conservatives, and there are thousands of people who did the same.

Some photos during my
modelling career

My wedding

**Top:** Julie with Horace Andy

**Middle:** Julie with singer Gregory Isaacs and producers

**Left:** Julie with Live Wyya

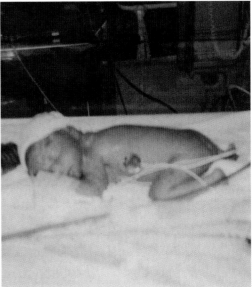

# Carnival princess, Jilly, joins the stars to boost charity cash

CARNIVAL queen Jilly Jones mixed with the stars at Notting Hill Carnival on Sunday, August 27, to raise money for cancer research.

The 10-year-old junior pupil collected more than £80 or charity by herself, dressed as a Caribbean princess at Europe's biggest street festival.

The Dowlais schoolgirl, rubbed shoulders with reggae star Finley Quaye and a host of DJs and appears during children's day at the annual carnival.

Jilly made her own costume and was sponsored by family members and friends to raise cash for the Cancer Research Western Union.

"It was all her own idea," said Jilly's mother Julie Jones. "A close friend of mine lost a son through cancer and Jilly feels very strongly about that.

"She went out there and raised every penny on her own."

Mrs Jones took her family to London for the 2 million-strong carnival because her children are part Afro-Caribbean and she likes them to learn about their cultures.

She said: "There were reggae floats, street bands and live stages but the children were more impressed with all the flamboyant costumes than with the stars dotted in the crowds and on the stages."

Last week Jilly's brother James, aged eight, scored a 1-0 win over Posh Spice Victoria Beckham when she spotted him wearing a Manchester United shirt in Cardiff.

She pointed him out as a true Beckham fan but saw the funny side when she realised he was wearing a Giggs top.

CARIBBEAN PRINCESS: Ten-year-old schoolgirl Jilly Jones meets reggae star Finley Quaye at the Notting Hill Carnival.

**Top Right:** Jilly Victoria Claire Jones born 7th January 1990

**Top Left:** Julie dining out

**Left:** Daughter Jilly with Finlay Quaye at Notting Hill Carnival

**Below:** Son James in the middle with his friends outside the Taj Mahal on the India Trip

**Top Left:** Julie with Rebecca, Jilly and James outside No. 10
**Top Right:** Julie and Jilly outside No. 10
**Bottom Left:** Julie with Sarah Brown inside No. 10
**Bottom Right:** The Brixton one pound note (front and back)

## *Monday 10th May 2010*

Still in the dark and stuck in a hung parliament. All parties have been locked in talks over the weekend and I am afraid it's up to Nick Clegg who runs our country and whether he decides to go in coalition with Labour or Conservative. I personally hope he will listen carefully to Labour's proposals as he should have done with the Conservatives and make his important decision.

Later this afternoon here we have breaking news, and to me very upsetting news, that Gordon Brown is to resign in the hope that the Lib Dems will work with Labour. He has sacrificed himself as Prime Minister in order for Labour to work in coalition with the Lib Dems. He is obviously putting our country first at this very difficult time; after all, no party in this election won an overall majority and this is why we are in a hung parliament. For the time being Gordon Brown has a constitutional right to stay Prime Minister until they can decide who is going to take over leadership of the Labour Party. Gordon Brown has behaved in a dignified manner and I personally pay tribute to his thirteen years in the Labour Party and the time he has spent in power. He didn't win the election on Thursday, but neither did the Conservative Party or the Lib Dems. I don't think that Gordon Brown should take this personally, because whoever was Prime Minister in a hung parliament, and especially this very complicated one, would be expected to resign. Gordon Brown has nothing to be ashamed of. He has had a remarkable career and said he would try his best for us, and he did. He had very good poll ratings during his time as Prime Minister. He grew up in a close-knit and loving family in Kirkcaldy, Scotland, and was a high achiever at school, studying politics at Edinburgh University. It is going to be very hard for him leaving Downing Street as he has been there for thirteen years, first as Chancellor, then as Prime Minister at Number 10. It was a life-long dream for him to become Prime Minister, and that dream came true. He did it as a driven, hard-working and dedicated politician and is stepping down as Prime Minister with dignity and no doubt great sadness.

## Tuesday 11th May 2010

Driving home at 8.45 pm, I stopped to get a coffee at McDonald's in Cardiff when I had a phone call from my daughter on my hands-free, informing me that David Cameron was the new Prime Minister. I told her she must be mistaken. The boy who served me my coffee at the drive-through overheard my conversation and I asked him whether it was true. He replied, "It better not be!" as he said his family came from a mining background. I switched on the radio immediately and heard that what my daughter had said was true: David Cameron was our new Prime Minister. I had tears in my eyes thinking of the Labour Party and Gordon Brown and his family, who had tried their utmost through the good and bad times. They had their trials and tribulations, their problems and their successes, and they should accept defeat with their heads high; after all, they still play a big part in fighting for our country. They will always have their supporters. It's a shame that not all of their supporters vote, and I am sure if they did they would never be out of power. I have spoken to lots of people who didn't vote, but when I explained a few things like what the Tories had planned such as cutting tax credits and taking the free TV licence from the over-75s etc. they said they would have definitely voted. I know that in the campaign trail Labour did their utmost to put their message across, but in a lot of the deprived areas many people didn't understand, and it takes ordinary people like us to spread the word.

The end of a sad day for me and thousands across Britain watching Gordon Brown and his family leave Downing Street. I wish him and his beloved wife and his two gorgeous little boys, John and Fraser, a wonderful future. I believe everything happens for a reason and hope now he can enjoy his family more without this gigantic weight on his shoulders. His children are still very young so he can now spend more quality time with them as they grow up. He is a devoted, caring and honourable father and husband, just as he was Prime Minister, and said that one thing which will never change is that he is Labour and Labour he will always be. I watched on the *BBC News* and cried as he made his statement that he was going to Her Majesty the Queen to tender his resignation and how he thanked his wife, Sarah, for her unwavering support and charity work. He also thanked his children for the love and joy they bring to their lives, and how he cherished first being a husband and father. I wish them happiness always. God bless them.

*JJ*

## 2010 World Cup, Rainbow Nation

What could be a more wonderful place to host the 2010 Football World Cup than "The Rainbow Nation", South Africa? I get very excited just thinking about it.

Every nationality in the world comes together and mixes in one spectacular event, watched the world over, with audiences reaching as high as 715 million people. They say football is the language of the world, and the Final itself is one of the most watched events in the world.

The legend, and, in many people's opinion, the greatest footballer to ever live, Pele, famously predicted many years ago that an African nation would win the World Cup by 2000. Whilst this didn't come true, the emerging African countries in the world football have opened the eyes of the world to the talent that exists. Premier League stars such as Emmanuel Adebayor, Michael Essien and Didier Drogba, three of the best players the League has to offer, all hail from Africa.

There are so many different cultures living in South Africa, now in harmony at last after all the nation has been through with the

Apartheid, which resulted in Nelson Mandela spending twenty-five years in prison. As we know, he came out of prison and went on to become the President of his beloved country.

We have fought so hard to 'kick racism out of football', so what better place to unite together for the pinnacle event in the sport, the World Cup. This is the nation of all people, as one, as God intended us to be.

South Africa is very proud to be hosting the event and is also proud of this new mantle bestowed upon it, "The Rainbow Nation", signifying every colour and creed as one. Cape Town is a beautiful city, albeit stricken by poverty, so I really hope the World Cup will not only boost tourism for the event, but increase the city's tourist industry long term by showing the world its splendour.

For the event itself, hundreds of thousands of fans over the month of June and into July will visit South Africa and this will boost the local economy hugely and showcase to the world what South Africa is all about.

England fans share a sense of expectation this summer and after the arrival of Fabio Capello, they are starting to believe they can go all the way. They begin against Algeria on 18 June in Cape Town. The success of fellow underachievers, Spain, in the last European Championships, only stokes the burning coals of hope more, and it is believed they have the talent and vision to bring the trophy back home for the first time since 1966. Who can forget England 4, West Germany 2, with my idol Sir Bobby holding aloft the Jules Rimet trophy to a packed Wembley Stadium alongside greats such as Sir Jack and Sir Bobby Charlton, Sir Geoff Hurst, Nobby Stiles MBE, and the rest of the legendary team?

South Africa is the first African nation to stage such a tournament, and this follows on from other recent global events that took place there. The British and Irish Lions recently toured South Africa, as did the England cricket team. Last year they also hosted the football

Confederations Cup, another huge event watched the world over and featuring teams like Spain and Brazil, Brazil going on to beat the USA in a great final.

Jacob Zuma, the current South African President, is proud to welcome the world and its fans to his country. I have heard that the people of Soweto have already invited fans and supporters to stay with them in a desperate bid to turn around the negative perceptions of their beloved country.

I was very sad to read about the shootings at the South Africa Cup of Nations in Angola which were targeting the Togo national team. I hope this does not deter anyone thinking of travelling to the World Cup. South Africa has already promised security will be at the forefront of their thinking and they guarantee a mass presence of security officers, coupled with intensive planning, to ensure the event goes ahead trouble-free. They also point out that we should not tar the continent of Africa as a whole because of one incident, and they consider South Africa in a better position than Angola to provide the kind of security level an event of this size warrants. If you are considering travelling, then do your homework before you go. Check the website fco.gov.uk/worldcup for helpful advice.

I hope everyone who travels from our "Great Mixed Nation" to South Africa's "Rainbow Nation" for the 2010 World Cup will have a wonderful time and a once-in-a-lifetime experience and, of course, good luck England!

Peace and God bless,

*JJ*


## Follow-up to the 2010 World Cup (Rainbow Nation)

Sunday 27th June 2010, a very sad day for England, beaten by Germany 4-1. While we have been full of hope and expectations only to be defeated in the worst possible way, I was shopping in Bristol, England, when I stopped to watch the game on a big screen. Tensions were high, a group of small children draped in a St George's flag, waiting for the next goal. Sadly, it didn't come from England. I couldn't help notice the tears running down a young lad's face, a man's face cupped in his hands and a woman sobbing uncontrollably. Although I am Welsh, I was supporting England and I was asked by a lady in the crowd why I was supporting England when I'm Welsh. I explained to her that after all, we are part of the United Kingdom, but if England were playing Wales, I would obviously support Wales. It made me think that yes, we should unite for the World Cup, instead of just England playing. We should all get together from our four great nations, England, Wales, Ireland and Scotland, and play united for Britain. This way the pressure wouldn't be all on England, we would have more choice with great players such as Robbie Keane (Ireland), Ryan Giggs (Wales), Darren Fletcher (Scotland) and, of course, David Beckham and so on for England. I think this would be only fair for Britain and it would stop all the controversy surrounding our other three nations feeling left out. I hope one day this will be the case. England needs our support more than ever; England's players are outstanding at club level but obviously under pressure when they are playing for their country. I feel Fabio Cappello made a mistake when he stopped the players' wives and girlfriends joining them for the World Cup as I feel if they had their partners' support it would have boosted their morale and their serotonin (the 'feel-good' hormone). It is also said that Cappello kept the players in suspense by not telling them which players were playing against Algeria until they actually got to the stadium. In my view, this only added to the tension, lowering their self-esteem, before they even started. Captain Steven Gerrard admitted defeat and held his hand up, saying they needed to basically play better and be more aggressive. On the other hand, Wayne Rooney reacted differently with their draw against Slovenia on

Monday 21st June 2010, letting out his frustration saying to the crowd, "It's nice to hear your own fans booing you." Some of the English fans were furious at this comment. I can understand this because it cost them a lot of money to get there and support their idols. I can also understand Rooney's frustration. I think he reacted not realising what he was saying. He hasn't long recovered from an ankle injury and must be so frustrated at not scoring when normally that's what he does best. To hear his own fans booing him must have felt like he was being kicked when he's down. I believe in sport you have to take the good with the bad. I think they should all stick together and rebuild on what they have got and learn by their mistakes, through the highs and lows and, with the support of their fans, they can do it. The other mistake I think Cappello made was that he was too quick to replace goalkeeper Robert Green after the draw with Slovenia. In my view he swapped players too frequently. I know Robert Green made an error but I believe because of his mistake he would have played better given the chance. He would have been more hungry to perform. David James, who replaced him, is generally a brilliant goalie, but changing players too often only adds to the problem in my view. I thought it was refreshing of Frank Lampard to back Wayne Rooney, saying that he is one of the best players in the world and how it must have been frustrating for him not to have scored goals in the World Cup. I believe that you can be the best sportsman in the world, whether it is a footballer, boxer, cricketer, etc., but if luck isn't on your side, despite being the best, you may not always win. So let's put this loss behind us, move forward and then enjoy the rest of the World Cup in South Africa. What moved me about the South African people is that when South Africa were knocked out of the World Cup they said that they were still winners in their eyes, regardless of their loss, and that they were still very proud to be hosting the 2010 World Cup. Because of this I believe they are winners all the way! Finally we have come to the end of the World Cup, which I am happy to announce that Spain have won – after all, this is the first time in history that they have won the World Cup. Viva España!

*JJ*

## Growing Up with a Deaf Mother

I got caught up in a conversation recently about someone growing up with a parent who is deaf and how they used sign language to communicate with each other, for which they had been taught. I sympathised with this person and could relate to them because my mother was deaf and it brought back lots of memories.

I have never really spoken about this before. I simply took it in my stride and got on with it because I didn't know any different, and I thought this was normal. During this conversation I couldn't help thinking that at least they could use sign language, which enabled them to talk and understand each other without struggling like we did as a family. I question why we never had the ability to talk with our mother. Nobody helped us and nobody was there to teach us. Why didn't the authorities help us? We were four children, three girls and a boy. My brother was the oldest and was always out. He did raise his voice a lot though, and now I understand why. Looking back, it was hard for us all. I also realise that there were far worse off families than ours, if that's any consolation. My father was always out working and then off to the pub. There was always a lot of noise in our house, especially where we'd have to shout or try to speak to our mother in a way that she could lip-read. I guess this may have been why our father would pack his bags and leave us on a regular basis, until my mother took us girls to follow him and bring him home; it was all so heartbreaking to witness. When I was a very small child of around four years old, my youngest sister was born. One day my aunt walked through the door to see me dragging on my mother's apron and uttering the words: "The baby is asking me to tell you she is crying." As young as I was, in my own way I was trying my hardest to get the message across. As the years went by we would sit down as a family and watch films together, and I remember my mother would love to watch 'the reading films' as we called them (subtitles). When there were no subtitles my older sister would literally sit through the film and explain every word and guide my mother through it; she would exaggerate her lip movements while speaking in order for my mother to understand. Whenever this didn't work she would then write it down for my mother to read. Looking back, my sister had great patience, because believe me, it was very hard trying to get my mother to understand us; we just learnt to make our own translations. On the other hand, I didn't have the same patience as my sister, and when my mother couldn't understand me I would shout it to her in the hope she would hear me, but she never did.

It must have been very difficult for my mother becoming deaf at the age of twenty-one whilst working in an ammunitions factory during the war; she always swore it was the noise in there that made her deaf.

My uncle, my mother's brother, took her to Harley Street in London where the top specialists in the world practise.

The hearing specialist there told her that she suffered from nervous deafness and she was given a special hearing aid so that, for example, if we knocked on the front door, she would feel the vibration and know we were there.

She was grateful that she could feel something; it was better than nothing, she always said.

While I was at school I must have raised my voice a lot without realising. I played for the school netball team in wing-attack. My sports teacher, Mrs Cole, gave me a few slaps on my legs that stung like hell. Other than that I haven't got a bad word to say about her, not that I'm condoning the slaps as it was before the ban on smacking in schools came into force. I guess it was a little too late for me.

The day came for me to leave school for good. Myself and all the other leavers were in the main hall having our last ever assembly when Mrs Cole singled me out and asked me, "Why didn't you tell me your mother was deaf?" I shrugged my shoulders and replied, "I didn't think I had to tell you, Miss." She said that if I had told her, I wouldn't have received so many slaps due to raising my voice. This is something that stuck in my mind and no doubt stuck with Mrs Cole for many years after. It's only now I am thinking back to how hard it was for us as a family to cope and how frustrating it was for our mother to communicate. I am glad that things have now changed, that the government helps people that are in the same situation we were in. I only wish we had this help. My mother passed away in her eighties, never regaining her hearing, but she took it in her stride and never complained about it once. R.I.P. Mam.

## *JJ*

## Chinese Culture in Britain

The Chinese people have been living in Britain since as far back as I can remember and brought a taste of China with them. The Chinese food and take-away business is and always has thrived, as it's one of Britain's favourite foods. When I was a child we had our very first Chinese restaurant (Hing Hong's) and believe me, it was a big treat to have a taste of another culture's cuisine, which was rare for our small valley, but nowadays they are more or less on every street corner. I remember around forty years ago a Chinese family arriving in our small town from Hong Kong. They brought along with them a fourteen-year-old son who explained to me that he felt isolated upon his arrival because Hong Kong was so busy and our valley was very quiet, not to mention the big culture shock and of course leaving behind the country which he grew up in and the friends and family he dearly loved. However, he settled into his new life very quickly indeed, doing well at school and helping out at his family restaurant. I must say that the people of our small town made them feel very welcome; after all, it was to be their home and they were about to open the first ever restaurant in our town which became an instant success. The menu boasted foods which we had never heard of or tasted as teenagers. I would go there with family and friends as it was the equivalent to a brassiere today, with a licensed bar in the corner of the restaurant and the luxurious Chinese décor which in those days we only ever saw in films. People would go there at the end of a night out from the pub; the place was full to capacity and the atmosphere was truly amazing. I am happy to have such memories we take for granted these days as more and more cultures mix together with an array of restaurants and take-aways from all over the world.

The same little boy who came here from Hong Kong when he was fourteen years old to a new world beyond his wildest dreams is still here to this day in the same little Welsh town he grew up in, continuing his family legacy by staying in the business all these years and making it his own. He married a Welsh lady and they have two beautiful inter-ethnic children who are achieving well academically and also help out in the business too.

In my late teens I went off to London to live. Whilst there I visited China Town and couldn't believe my eyes at all the wonderful Chinese restaurants and street décor. There I was thinking that this small but amazing business which had opened up in my town was a wonderful and rare luxury for us, yet two hundred miles away in this country there was a whole community dedicated to the Chinese culture. With Chinese restaurants everywhere, groceries, clothing, ornaments and everything you could think of from the Chinese culture and here we have it: China Town, Soho, London. China Town brings major tourism to Britain.

Chinese history in this country goes back to the early 19th century when many Chinese people came here, settling mainly in our big cities, with the Chinese people contributing largely to our economic growth. They also have one of the highest inter-ethnic relationship rates in Britain and are known to be one of the highest achievers academically.

## *JJ*

The boy who came to Britain from Hong Kong, now a man with his daughter.

## WAGs Bickering over Parking Fines!

You don't have to be a WAG to get parking fines; believe me, I should know. I also should be ashamed to say it, but it's true. I read a recent press article that Danielle Lloyd was discussing Alex Curran pictured getting yet another parking fine. I can understand Danielle's comments that Alex shouldn't waste money, and I know too well Danielle is right in saying you don't know what's around the corner, that one day there may not be any money, so why waste it on parking fines? But maybe Alex is thinking literally what or who is around the corner when she parks on double yellows like the paparazzi, or even robbers and stalkers, etc. I know this is no excuse to continually park illegally, but this could be one of the many reasons to get in and out of whatever she has to do quickly. After all, she has been through a very scary time with her home being burgled whilst her and her two children were present.

The reason I say I should know and can relate to this is because I've had so many parking fines and should be ashamed of myself. I urge anyone reading this to take heed as I have had bailiffs knocking on my door, even taking my furniture out onto the pavement and my car clamped until finally I paid up to a thousand pounds for three parking fines that accumulated over a period of time. I was devastated when the bailiffs called and embarrassed me in front of my neighbours, and all for something as self-inflicting as parking fines and even congestion charges, as the famous chart-topping rapper Dizzee Rascal mentions in his song "Road Rage". One bailiff that I tricked (well, I thought I tricked) had his own back on me, big time! I agreed to pay him over the phone at a specific date but in the meantime I filled in a time-to-pay TE9 form from the court and the court agreed for me to pay the original fines instead of the bailiff's fees of a thousand pounds. More fool me, I was even late paying that. So here comes the bailiff knocking on my door again; this time he was back with a vengeance. I eventually come out of my house, quickly locking the door behind me while he sat waiting in his car, knowing that if he had put his foot over my threshold he would have been in and there would have been nothing I could do about that by law. He was furious; I got in my car along with my friend and the chase was on! He chased us around the streets; it was so embarrassing with everyone out on their doorsteps looking and wondering what was going on.

At the time there were builders in the street. They even tried to block him so that he couldn't catch up with me, and they had to jump out of the way as he almost ran them over.

Concerned about the builders getting hurt through their kindness towards me, I quickly stopped my car and surrendered. The bailiff immediately clamped my car. I was furious and told him that he may have clamped my car but he was not getting into my house! He went around to my garden and realising that I had not locked my back door I thought, "Sh*t, I've had it." The bailiff was in my house starting to remove my television sets, coffee tables, furniture, etc. I realised I was in a no-win situation.

I paid him a few pennies short of a thousand pounds. While I wrote him a cheque, his face was beaming, as if to say "Yes, that's right I've had you", and this is why I feel Danielle Lloyd has a big point in what she's saying.

When I read it I couldn't help thinking of my situation and I'm ashamed to say that I've had hundreds of parking fines and congestion charges and various bailiffs knocking at my door. This is just one instance I've chosen to discuss.

I know bailiffs have a job to do and there are rules that once they're in your home there's nothing you can do about it unless you pay your debt to them.

Some bailiffs will give you a chance and time to pay by taking a list of your chattels; others won't give you that chance, but they can't break into your house, that is illegal.

Later that day, curious that the bailiff had chased me around the streets, I phoned the bailiffs complaints office. They told me that he was wrong to chase me and that I could have taken the matter further, but I decided to let it go as I thought he's paid, he's gone and I just have to make sure he never comes back. My advice to anyone who is tempted to park illegally, even if it's for a few, just a few minutes, is DON'T. Think first.

This is why I know you don't have to be a WAG to get parking fines. In the mid-eighties I met the football megastar George Best in Blushies wine bar on the Kings Road, London. He was simply standing by the bar, when he asked me out for dinner. He was one of the nicest people I have ever met in my life and he commented on my green eyes, but he had the most piercing blue eyes I have ever seen. I declined his offer because I had a boyfriend at the time; after all, I could have been one of the biggest WAGs of all time, if I had taken up his offer.

Rest in peace George Best

*JJ*

# Rugby Culture in Wales

I have grown up in a rugby cultured family; my father practically lived and breathed for the game. He came from a Welsh-speaking town, Llanelli in Mid-Wales, whose stadium, Straddy Park, is known worldwide.

My father was very proud of his rugby roots and loved playing as a youth. In an odd sort of way you could say he died for the game, literally. He followed his beloved Wales every game he could, until one evening travelling home from Cardiff Arms Park where Wales triumphed over England by winning 6-nil! He was in an ecstatic mood and celebrated this great victory. Travelling home after this wonderful evening he was tragically knocked down by a drunk driver, putting him in a coma. He later died of his injuries.

I'm finding it very difficult to write this column as it's bringing back so many memories of that fatal night. My father would have been curious to see how the rugby culture has changed in Wales and how more and more people from all backgrounds enjoy rugby, especially women. The sport is not so male dominated any more, with Welsh women dressing up in Welsh costumes and rugby kits to make a big day of it, whether it's at the game in the stadium or at home or watching it on the big screen at the pub.

It's a big day for our girls of all ages in Wales; it seems they can't wait for the next international. Our pubs, restaurants, clubs are full to capacity at these times, the atmosphere is electric. Our very own Welsh film superstar, Richard Burton, was a true rugby fan and former player. He once made a statement that he would rather play for Wales in Cardiff Arms Park than appear in Shakespeare at London's Old Vic Theatre; but then Richard Burton was a true Welshman.

When I was growing up I can remember great players such as Gareth Edwards, Barry John and J. P. R. Williams, and of course the one and only Ray Gravell. Rugby is a huge part of Welsh culture and it's here to stay. It's just that the culture's changed and more women are involved.

Many years ago women didn't join in, but secretly the adrenaline must have been pumping through their veins and nowadays they can openly enjoy a part of Welsh history that's here forever. "COME ON WALES!"

After my father's death, for his dedication to rugby, he had a rugby cup honoured in his name, which belongs to a Welsh rugby club and is always awarded to the winning team, even to this day. The cup is named after my father, 'The Tommy Cisco Cup'. The name 'Cisco' was a nick-name given to my father in the army because he very much resembled the actor Cesar Romero, from the film 'The Cisco Kid'. My father would have been very proud of this honour awarded to him in his memory for his life-long support and dedication to Welsh rugby.

R.I.P. Dad

I would like to pay tribute to British Rugby commentator Bill McLaren, who sadly passed away at the age of 86 in 2010. Bill was the voice of rugby; he was a BBC broadcaster for almost half a century.

R.I.P. Bill McLaren

I would also like to pay tribute to our very own Ray Gravell, a rugby genius, who played rugby for Llanelli R.F.C. in the '70s, leading on to an international level, earning 23 caps for Wales. He was also chosen for the 1980 British Lions Tour in South Africa. He was truly loved by rugby fans all over Wales, and no doubt worldwide. His funeral can only be described as that of a state funeral at his beloved Straddy Park.

R.I.P. Ray Gravell

*JJ*

# Premature Birth

My first child was born prematurely, weighing just 3lb 7oz. When I held her literally in the palm of my hand, her tiny head fitted around my hand while her body fitted comfortably around my wrist. I was thirty-three years old when I became a mother for the first time. Because of my age, I had taken extra precautions, making sure I ate healthy food and took vitamins; you name it, I did it if it was healthy.

I underwent all the tests needed, especially as I was an older mum; one test came back showing concern regarding spina bifida. I had to go to the University of Wales Hospital for checks. The doctors there offered me an amniocentesis, which involves injecting a needle into the uterus to draw fluid from the unborn child to check the baby is 100% fine. I was offered counselling first and decided against this method because the counsellor explained to me that there was a chance the baby could abort, but that chance was far too great. Leaving the hospital bewildered and distraught, I made an appointment for further tests, including another ultra-sound scan. The doctor did more extensive checks and advised me that he felt the baby was fine. I took his advice, along with my decision not to have the amniocentesis and carry on with the pregnancy.

I must admit, I had concerns over my baby's health. I had almost two months to go until the birth, when driving home one evening my waters broke in my car. I wondered what on earth was happening to me and immediately drove to the local hospital, where they kept me in overnight, explaining to me that they would allow the labour to progress and when the baby was born, because the lungs would not be fully developed, they would do everything they could to save the baby after I gave birth. Luckily for me, I didn't go into labour after all and left the hospital the next day.

Two weeks later and still not into my full nine months of pregnancy, I went into labour. This time I was prepared and packed my overnight bag, making my way to the hospital where I had initially booked. My gynaecologist at this hospital did the complete opposite to what the previous hospital was going to do, explaining to me that because I was going to have a premature baby and that the baby's lungs had not yet fully developed, he would give me an injection to develop the lungs while the baby was still in my womb. In other words, he fought for my baby's life while she was still inside me, rather than wait for the birth and then fight for my baby's life. I couldn't understand how two hospitals could follow two very different procedures. The second option sounded a lot better to me, and I shudder to think what would have happened if I had given birth in the first hospital. I would have thought that to save the baby whilst still inside me was a much better option than to wait until the baby was born, especially with something as serious as undeveloped lungs. I was advised that the baby would have breathing complications when born. After eight hours and an epidural, my baby girl was born perfectly healthy and without breathing complications at all due to the professionalism and the decisions of the gynaecologist. She may have only been three pounds seven ounces, but she was perfect.

The first thing I asked the midwife was if her spine was okay because of the previous scare I had had when I was offered the amniocentesis. My baby had to stay in Special Care for many weeks, and because the hospital was twenty-five miles away from our local hospital, she had to be transferred to the Special Care Unit there. I wasn't allowed to travel with her in the ambulance because she was still in an incubator. She had her own nurse while travelling, whilst I travelled with my family in a car behind.

When we reached the local Special Care Unit the nurses were waiting for her arrival. I asked the nurse if my baby was okay travelling and she explained that she was fine, just that her blood pressure had risen slightly. I was all questions when she told me this, and she explained that because the baby had been in a calm environment for so long, the change and travelling might have alarmed her a little. I thought to myself, as small as my baby is and just a few weeks old, she can still feel that something is going on. I thanked the nurses and all the staff for everything they had done, they were absolutely wonderful.

My baby stayed in Special Care for a few more weeks. The doctors asked me about how I felt about taking such a small baby home, as I could have waited a little longer if I wasn't ready, but I couldn't wait to take her home. I feel it is a mother's instinct to handle her baby, never mind how small. I just followed that.

The doctors also informed me that she had a Mongolian blue spot on the bottom of her back, which could be linked to her being of mixed-race origin, and I was intrigued by this. Mongolian blue spots are more common in darker skinned people, e.g. those of African and Asian descent, and my child was one of the 90% of darker skinned children who develop one. Darker skinned people produce more melanin; this is one reason why they are more common in darker skin. Mongolian blue spots form when melanocytes, which are skin cells within the skin that produce the pigment melanin, become trapped as the baby grows inside the womb. My baby may have been a premature baby but there were no complications or problems, and she has been a healthy child growing up. As for the Mongolian blue spot, it has never been a problem; in fact, at twenty years of age, only now is she finding out she has one.

*JJ*

## Thank God for my Child

My baby was prem,
She is such a gem,
As light as a feather,
But thank God we're together.
I nearly did lose her,
But she clung to my flesh,
She could not cling no more,
So she opened the door.
They fought for her life,
While still in my womb,
As I looked around,
The darkened room,
I prayed to God,
That she would survive,
And now my darling daughter's happy and alive.

Author Julie Rice Jones

## Notting Hill Carnival

For many years I took my children to London to visit Notting Hill Carnival on August Bank Holiday weekend. I felt that my children could embrace their culture, and what better way to experience a part of their heritage than at the Notting Hill Carnival.

In the last few years I have noticed that it has become a lot more cosmopolitan. Many years ago, when my children were very young, it was all about the Caribbean culture, but now all cultures are integrating and joining in at this wonderful event, which proves our country is becoming an ever-growing melting pot, with not only Caribbean food being served on every corner, as it was years ago, but also foods from all over the world, including Mexican, Spanish, Brazilian… you name it, it's there. The same goes for the music, with Reggae, Calypso, Soca and Ska, etc.

I would take my children up to the event on a Sunday, as it is Children's Day, and millions of people would join in. We would rub shoulders with the stars. There were Reggae floats and street bands but my children were more impressed with all the flamboyant costumes than the stars. One year we spent the day with the Reggae star Finley Quaye. He was so protective of the children and so friendly, the atmosphere was amazing. To me the Notting Hill Carnival is a celebration of the Caribbean culture; however, everybody is welcome. Jamelia has performed at Notting Hill Carnival. The Carnival began in the 1960s with the first Notting Hill Carnival in 1966, and it has been held every year since. It is the second biggest street carnival in the world, with the Trinidad and Tobago Carnival being the first. People travel from all over the world to attend the Notting Hill Carnival to enjoy the experience, with every culture on the planet mixing as one. No doubt the Notting Hill Carnival will go down in history and I hope it will continue forever more so that my grandchildren and great-grandchildren can experience what my children and I have.

## JJ

## Premiership Footballer Emmanuel Adebayor and his 'Gun T-shirt'

I mentioned in one of my previous columns how football icon Emmanuel Adebayor and his Togo team mates were shot at during the 2010 African Nations Cup. I thank God he is still alive as he is such a world-class footballer and seems to be a great person too.

However, I cannot understand why he was recently seen wearing a T-shirt featuring a gun. In my and many other people's eyes, that is just like promoting the thing that so very nearly killed him and his fellow players. Some of his fellow passengers on that bus were not so lucky. His coach driver, assistant manager and PR man were all shot dead in the horrendous attack. Adebayor and the Togo team were all so shocked by the attack which occurred in the host nation of the cup, Angola, that they decided to withdraw from the competition entirely, fearing for their safety. Abebayor, Captain of the Togo team and a Manchester City player, was so devastated by the attack at the time and he was honoured by the decision of his colleagues to play a match in memoriam of those who lost their lives at the hands of the gunmen. He was quoted as saying that death was the most horrific thing he had ever witnessed, yet in March 2010, just two months after the shootings, he was sighted at the MEN Arena in Manchester at a 50 Cent gig wearing this offensive T-shirt. 50 Cent himself was shot nine times and the way he deals with this is by rapping about it through his lyrics.

I can understand where 50 Cent is coming from, but I cannot understand why Adebayor chose to wear a T-shirt promoting a gun so soon after the shootings. What would the family of those who sadly died in January 2010 have thought of this public display? A sports star of his stature has his every move watched and debated, the eyes of the world are upon you when you're at the top of your profession, and with that comes great responsibility. I personally feel he should have been more sensitive, if not to himself and his close circle, then to the millions of teenagers, my son included, who look up to him as an idol, a role model. With gun crime rates soaring in our inner cities, this kind of display was not warranted and is the last thing we need in the fight to remove trouble from our streets and our lives.

*JJ*

## Help us Fight Leukaemia – We Need More Bone Marrow Donors

I was shocked and very upset to discover that there are fewer suitable bone marrow donors for ethnic and mixed race people who suffer from leukaemia. There is a 1 in 5 chance of a Northern European finding a bone marrow match, compared with a 1 in 100,000 chance for black, ethnic and mixed race people. This extraordinary disparity in chance comes from the fact that, unlike blood donation, bone marrow donation is race-related. Before a bone marrow transplant is considered, all other options, like chemotherapy, are exhausted first.

It's heartbreaking to hear that many people have died because they couldn't find a donor with the same ethnic background. My children are both mixed race and I fear what would happen if they developed leukaemia. I urge in the strongest sense more black and mixed race people to become bone marrow donors – they could save so many more lives.

I know part of the problem is a lack of understanding within the community, and despite being a mother to mixed race children, only now have I come to realise the depth and impact this issue may have. I think if more people were alerted to these shocking statistics, then we would see a lot more people coming forward to donate, and I implore you to do so.

I was inspired by the story of Karla Neckles. Karla died in 2009 of leukaemia, but the most poignant and tragic aspect of her story was that she was just weeks away from undergoing her transplant operation. After an arduous and desperate search for a donor since being diagnosed with leukaemia, Karla eventually found a donor in Germany but sadly passed away before the operation could take place. Karla, like many others of mixed race, found her options and chance of survival extremely limited as she found the odds were heavily stacked against her due to her race. Heartbreakingly, Karla, aged just twenty-one, left behind two young children who will now grow up without their loving mother.

The African-Caribbean Leukaemia Trust, or the ACLT, is a charity set up in 1996 by Beverley De-Gale and Orin Lewis to promote bone marrow or blood donation. They were the parents of former leukaemia sufferer Daniel De-Gale, and he inspired them to do all they could to help other people with leukaemia.

The ACLT was initially set up when Daniel had already suffered with leukaemia for three years. Daniel's parents were told that his only hope of survival was to receive a bone marrow transplant from someone within the black community, as bone marrow contains racially specific characteristics. At that time, there were only 550 black or mixed race people on the donor list in the UK. The consultant at Great Ormond Street who was responsible for Daniel's treatment informed his parents that there was just an approximate 1 in 250,000 chance of Daniel finding a compatible donor. Can you imagine how you would feel as a parent being told your son had only a one in a quarter of a million chance of survival?

As I mentioned earlier, the first stage of increasing the chances of black or mixed race people fighting this disease is to increase awareness of the shortfall of odds in their favour. The ACLT charity wishes to highlight the problem, so as to encourage more people to step forward and donate. I hope I can help the ACLT by raising awareness through this column.

Recruiting more donors through the ACLT registration clinics offers a glimmer of hope to people who find themselves at odds, with a slim chance of survival, delivering hope of a healthy future to people whose illnesses would otherwise prove to be fatal. Bone marrow is a blood-like liquid which can be donated from one person to another in one of two simple procedures.

In 1999, Daniel's parents were informed that a matching unrelated donor had been found on 16th June that year, and Daniel received a bone marrow transplant at Great Ormond Street Hospital. At twelve years old, Daniel was in remission for nine years, and he went on to attend university and pursued the normal life that many people of his age take for granted. Unfortunately, Daniel lost his fight with cancer as complications with Daniel's health led to multiple organ failure and he died at the tender age of twenty-one on 8th October 2008 in hospital, surrounded by his family. Daniel may not have had many years in his life, but plenty of life in his years. He was inspired by many to make a difference, which is why we must all support his legacy by backing the ACLT in its aims to save more lives.

Many sufferers and their families contact the ACLT from the UK and indeed around the world, asking for their help with donor appeals, providing advice, raising awareness and recruiting people to be suitable potential donors. Unfortunately, at any given time around 7000 people require life-saving bone marrow transplants, and to make this even more difficult, only 3% of potential donors are made up of ethnic minorities.

This is why it is imperative that the ACLT receives all the public and financial support it can get to save more lives. By promoting this worthy charity, we can help them continue to promote successful bone marrow and blood donation throughout the UK and worldwide to give hope to all leukaemia and bone marrow cancer sufferers of all racial backgrounds. People of black and mixed race blood deserve to have the same help and chances of survival as anyone else.

Orin Lewis and Beverley De-Gale are the co-founders, chief executive and manager of the ACLT. They explain that they witness families fighting with tremendous courage and strength and stress that they do not want this battle to be in vain.

The patrons of the ACLT are the Duchess of York, former Sugababe Keisha Buchanan, premiership footballer Micah Richards, world heavyweight boxing champion David Haye, actor Colin Salmon and ex-international footballing superstar John Barnes. These instantly recognisable stars act as ambassadors for the charity and help to raise awareness through their work for the ACLT. John Barnes, for example, attended a recent 'Gift of Life' Ball in London, a fundraising event.

For further information about registering a potential bone marrow or blood donor or to find out about up-and-coming registration drives, please contact the charity on 0208 2404480, email them at info@aclt.org or visit the website at www.aclt.org.

Show an interest, spread the word and make a difference.

Thank you.

*JJ*

## Domestic Violence

Unfortunately, domestic violence is a very sad and active part of our society. Many years ago, women in violent relationships or marriages would remain silent about abuse and the violence they endured and simply put up with it. In the past it was looked upon as a stigma and a failure on the woman's part if the marriage broke down.

Sadly, even these days, it still goes on, and many women choose to keep quiet about the abuse, just putting up with and accepting it as an inevitability. It takes a lot of courage to stand up to this abuse and break free from a lifestyle that they have become accustomed to. Despite it making them feel miserable and deeply unhappy with their life, they can feel that there's no way out, but there is.

I am a firm believer that everyone deserves a second chance, but second is second, and when it develops into a third, fourth or fifth chance, then we have a problem that has fully developed and is now a major issue that shows no sign of disappearing.

The worst thing you can do is to hide your abuser and shelter them, because then they feel free to abuse you even more, safe from prying eyes that are not on them or ready to step in and stop them at any time. You would, in fact, be giving them the environment in which to pursue this abuse. It is important to remember that abuse doesn't necessarily have to be physical, it can be mental and emotional too, which can be just as, if not more, damaging.

I personally went through this myself some years ago. It started inconspicuously enough, being picked on here and there for no reason. It then became more frequent and intense, forcing me to walk on egg shells all of the time, worrying constantly what kind of mood he would come home in, not being able to let my guard down and wondering when I was going to 'get it' again.

This lowered my self-esteem to unbearable levels, made me feel vulnerable and inadequate. I just wanted a content and peaceful life. Just because it wasn't physical abuse, I felt I had no option other than to put up with it.

It came to a stage where I couldn't take it anymore, and I was sick of being treated as a doormat. So I left.

It was heartbreaking leaving, with all kinds of mixed emotions running through my head, all the 'what if' and 'if only' thoughts making me question the move and if it was the right choice. It is always important to remember that when you begin a relationship with someone, it would have felt right at the start, so to question if it's right now is only natural. But you have to let your head rule your heart, and make a decision which is unquestionably the right one.

Leaving a relationship like this really did feel like a massive weight being lifted off my shoulders. Believe me, time IS the biggest healer. At first you think you will never get over it, but time fixes everything.

All relationships have their ups and downs and yes, you do have to work at it together to overcome any hurdles. But if there is physical or emotional abuse involved, it's time to seriously start thinking about your future and your safety.

I know it's easier said than done, especially when there are children involved, but there is help and support out there for women and their children, and indeed men also, who are suffering from domestic abuse. It is important to understand that while this problem is traditionally associated with women getting abused, especially in the old days, nowadays many men suffer domestic abuse as well.

There is an organisation called Women's Aid which helps women and men, along with their children, who are victims of domestic abuse and helps them to break free from it. They have facilities and accommodation for those who need it all over Britain.

If you have been the victim of domestic abuse you can call the Women's Aid national helpline on 0808 2000 247.

## *JJ*

## Knife Crime in Britain

Yet another tragic story appears in the news – a young person has been stabbed to death. A headline that appears all too frequently these days.

Some people have admitted to me that they have carried a knife, but for their protection. Not to use it, but to have it on them to deter anyone from attacking them. Simply carrying one at all could lead to it being used, and to kill someone, you have to think about the consequences. Today there are more and more people being stabbed in the inner cities of Britain than ever before.

I remember years ago my brother came home with a black eye and a bloodied face after being punched in a fight. My mother started crying and pleading with him to tell her what had happened, but he just sat there and didn't say anything. We were all shocked and upset as a family at this attack, but can you imagine if he had been stabbed in the fight?

In times gone by, they would use only their fists, which I am not condoning for one second, but these days it's much more likely to be knives or weapons used in fights. I have a teenage son myself and cannot sleep when he is on a night out until I hear that key turning in the door upon his return. It is every parent's worst nightmare for something to happen to their children and many have told me they also lie awake waiting for the children to return home safe.

But we also have to let go to a certain extent and let them explore their own lives, and that comes with dangers. There is so much to experience out there which is good, and not everything is bad with the world. I always preach to my son to keep out of trouble, walk or run away from it, which always takes the bigger man.

Here are just some of the young children that have been killed by knife crime within the UK:

Damilola Taylor was stabbed to death ten years ago in the hallway of the block of flats where he lived. He was just ten years old.

Ben Kinsella, brother of the actress Brooke Kinsella, the *EastEnder*'s star, was only sixteen when he was stabbed to death.

Sofyen Belamouadden was just fifteen when he was killed after a stabbing at Victoria Station.

The list, sadly, goes on and on.

In 2008, the *Daily Mirror* organised a march titled 'Stop Knives, Save Lives' which raised awareness and helped to provide a support network for people affected. You can join Families UTD which was set up to combat knife crime through their website or through Facebook. The *Daily Mirror* states that the website will contain advice, routes to support and testimonials from families and communities affected by knife crime.

To carry a knife and commit knife crime you will also be committing yourself to being locked up in prison and paying the consequences of your thoughtless actions. Your whole life can be thrown away in one senseless act. It is the parents of victims who are left devastated. Remember, it's someone's child you are attacking. Imagine how your parents would feel if they lost you in a murder.

I preach to my son, and I preach to you all, don't carry a knife. If you don't have one on you, one won't be used, and the waste of life for everyone involved, be it the victim, the victim's family or even your own as punishment, will be avoided. Think before you act.

*JJ*

## The Ministerial Debate/The Campaign Trail

I have been watching with great interest the run-up to the election and like thousands of people across Britain couldn't wait for the BBC's ministerial debates. I wasn't interested in politics when I was younger but find myself very interested as I have got older. After all, politics decide the future of our nation. I am a Labour supporter but couldn't help admire all three politicians, Gordon Brown, Nick Clegg and David Cameron. They are three very powerful men and it is overwhelming to just think that our future depends on them. All three want to fight tooth and nail for our country regardless of their differences and policies. I have no doubt in my mind that Gordon Brown's policies are strongest. I also believe in the old saying 'better the devil you know', and why change now when Gordon Brown is getting us out of recession?

In my opinion, the debate itself was amazingly captivating politics, the first in British history. This gives everybody, especially young people, and people who may not have voted at all, a chance to see these three politicians speaking for ninety minutes and to choose who they feel is the man for the job. I was sitting on egg shells watching the programme in case one of the leaders stumbled on their words, but not one of them did; after all, this was a live television debate and the first ever one.

The United States of America are used to having these televised debates and have done for years. I have seen some of the debates and was impressed with the Obama debate and the J F Kennedy debate. I can honestly say that regardless of the outcome on 7th May 2010, I feel proud to be part of a country where three powerful leaders took part in the first ever debate in Britain with such power, charm, style and charisma. It will go down in history that they played such a role in a fascinating and entertaining debate. Although there may be concerns that some people will be influenced by style over substance, people have to remember that it's not a beauty contest, it's serious politics. I have spoken to some girlfriends of mine who explained to me that since watching the debate they are definitely going to vote, some for the first time. After all, one hundred years ago, Emmeline Pankhurst was jailed for fighting for the right for women to vote, so we owe it to her.

I think all this nonsense about who is the youngest, who is the better-looking, etc. is ridiculous. After all, Winston Churchill didn't have youth on his side when he was Prime Minister but was one of the best Prime Ministers we ever had, taking us to victory over Germany in the war in 1944. On this subject I must say that Gordon Brown does not look his fifty-nine years, I would take at least ten years off that. I think the campaign trail has gone well for all three parties, apart from a few hiccups and hecklers. I was worried for their safety at such an important time in politics and I thank God no-one was hurt. Gordon Brown did find himself in a very bad situation when confronted by a sixty-six-year-old pensioner, Mrs Duffy. I watched as she tackled Mr Brown on immigration and the Prime Minister was overheard calling her a bigot. He apologised to Mrs Duffy, who is a Labour supporter. He explained the whole situation was misunderstood and Mrs Duffy accepted his apology. Sometimes we all say things under pressure and off the slip of the tongue, not meaning to upset or offend. The most important thing is to admit that you're wrong and accept responsibility and, of course, to apologise.

I am aware that immigration is out of control but our government are doing their best to bring it down. They are using a points system, just like Australia. It has to be dealt with strictly and fairly because after all, we are part of the European Union and thousands of Britons want the chance to live abroad too; it is one of Gordon Brown's top priorities. At least one good thing is that regardless of each party's policies and differences, I am happy that they agreed to disagree with any questions and answers from the BNP. I watched the Welsh debates and couldn't have felt more proud that the parties stuck together when the BNP put questions forward. I felt especially proud of Peter Hain, the Welsh Secretary who stands for Labour, when he made it clear that he would have nothing to do with the BNP and any of their questions, especially as the BNP had made a statement in the past saying there is no such thing as a black Welshman. As Peter Hain stated in the Welsh debate, "What about Colin Jackson?" The BNP are exploiting the immigration system and using it to their advantage and to promote their racist views. Let's not fall for it.

In the third and final debate the issue of how good schooling starts in nursery and primary years arose, yet Conservatives and Liberals want to cut Child Tax Credit for these very children, so how can they help deprived areas if they plan to do this? All through the three debates not once was it mentioned that the Labour government have put in resources for breakfast clubs so that every child can have breakfast enhancing their performance, especially in deprived areas of Britain. After all, these children are our future; one of them is going to be Prime Minister one day. The breakfast clubs also make it easier for single parents and married couples to go off to work.

Along with many other priorities on Gordon Brown's list are the elderly. He said we have to give our old people dignity and security in old age. I am writing this column on May Bank Holiday Monday 2010 with only four days to go before we can vote. I hope Gordon Brown will still be Prime Minister on 7th May. I know one thing, Gordon Brown has two new voters: my children, who have reached the age where they can vote and choose for themselves, and they have: LABOUR!

*JJ*

## Tribute to a Legend, Gregory Isaacs

I would like to wish all our readers of *The Big Eye* newspaper a very happy Christmas, although for some, it's a sad time, especially those who have lost their loved ones. My heart goes out to them.

Gregory Isaacs sadly passed away on 10th October in London, and I would like to pay tribute to a legend. I was lucky enough to have met him; it was such an honour for me. We met when he was performing at Q bar in Cardiff in 2008. I wrote a story about his show for the *The Big Eye*, explaining how the crowd erupted when Gregory belted out one of his most famous songs, "Night Nurse". I found Gregory to be an honourable and cool character; I can understand why they called him 'the cool ruler'. He had an aura about him and reassured me he would be back in Cardiff for one day to do another show. Sadly, that was never meant to be.

Gregory also performed in Cardiff twenty-five years ago at Sophia Gardens alongside Misty and Roots, Aswad and The Specials at the very special event entitled 'Rock Against Racism'.

I and many others would like to thank Gregory Isaacs for bringing Reggae music into our homes, lives and hearts, and for inspiring us with his lyrics.

He has left us to join legends such as Bob Marley and Dennis Brown. No doubt the three of them will be jamming, bringing joy in heaven as they did on earth. We will go on forever buying their music; they were gifted geniuses.

Gregory was born in Kingston and went on to become one of the world's greatest Reggae artists of all time. Gregory told me how he loved the UK but worshipped his beloved homeland, Jamaica. I myself feel proud to have met him. I also feel proud to have resided in Kingston and visited his place of birth, along with other ghetto areas including Trenchtown, Brownstown and Waterhouse. Some of the nicest people I have met came from the ghetto. There are a lot of talented people there, especially musical talent, and I have noticed the most beautiful women come from the ghetto. They are very proud people and don't expect handouts. They just want the chance to make it themselves – 'a break', that's all. I know these areas have their problems like everywhere but these people deserve a chance, you only have to look in the ghetto to find this talent.

Kingston is the root, the home and the heart of Reggae music, and we around the world love it. There are an enormous amount of potential artists in Kingston and we need this talent. I hope one day these people get the chance they deserve, and let's hope that their talent will not go unsung and go on to create many more talented geniuses like Gregory Isaacs. We will miss Gregory greatly, but he will live on through his music. My heart goes out to his family at this very sad time.

R.I.P. GREGORY ISAACS

*JJ*

## 2018 World Cup Bid

It's 14.45 on Thursday 2nd December 2010, with most of the UK snowed in under freezing temperatures. I, along with many more across the country, cannot think of a better way to spend the day than holed up at home, watching the outcome of who gets to host the 2018 World Cup. I'm glued to the television screen, eagerly awaiting the outcome on which so much depends.

The result is going to be later than expected, as the twenty-two FIFA delegates are voting in private. Tensions are running high as thousands have braved the weather to turn out in support of England's bid, young and old gathered in unison at City Hall in London, the historic Tower of London in the backdrop. Across the country, many more thousands gather in Liverpool, Manchester, Birmingham – everywhere across the country.

It's now 14.53, and still no decision. How much longer? At 15.28, Jérôme Valcke, the General Secretary of FIFA, is on stage and ready to announce the winner. He describes England as having a remarkable bid, and says that in football we learn to win, which is easy, but we also learn to lose, which is not so easy. He refers to England as "the motherland of football"; high praise indeed, things are looking promising.

Then, at 15.37 UK time, he opens the envelope and announces to the waiting world, that Russia has won the right to host the 2018 World Cup.

My heart, and millions more, sinks.

The crowds gathered across Britain silently disperse and go their separate ways. These people expected a carnival atmosphere, a party that would go on well into the night as jubilant English football fans celebrated a momentous coup for the country. A party like the scenes at Trafalgar Square in 2005 when it was announced we had won the bid to host the 2012 Olympics. But it was not to be.

I remembered the jubilation and euphoria when South Africa won the right to host the last World Cup and I wanted to experience that feeling myself. I vividly remember the look of utter dejection on Alan Shearer's face as the result sank in.

If we couldn't win with the backing of our Prime Minister and Prince William, then it's fair to say we couldn't have won at all. I know it's hard but we have to remain positive that we have had the World Cup before; not only that, we won it when it was here, and there will be another chance, another time in the future, as distant as it may seem.

Alan Shearer, when discussing the outcome, admitted it was devastating and hard to swallow, but in an act of dignified British behaviour, ensured he congratulated Russia for their success. We are the greatest footballing nation in the world, with arguably the best league, but we are also a very supportive nation, who will congratulate the winners and take the losses as we take the wins, with dignity.

David Beckham made a statement saying we didn't get enough votes from the FIFA members, and paid tribute to the bid team. One thing is for sure, he couldn't have done more for the bid. Whenever it was mentioned on TV, there was Beckham, working tirelessly in the aim of bringing the World Cup home. Qatar were surprising hosts for the 2022 World Cup and I do not think many people could have called that outcome, but Beckham congratulated them also on a remarkable achievement.

He went on to explain that football was in our DNA in this country, and what a great place it would have been to host the World Cup. We have the infrastructure, the supporters, the venues and transport to ensure it would have been a complete success. Prince William, who also worked tirelessly on promoting the bid, said he loves football, and that the game truly did bring people together from all backgrounds and cultures.

Football and support worker Eddie Afekafe, who worked side by side with Prince William, the Prime Minister and David Beckham, stole the show in my eyes. He gave me goose bumps when he told of how he grew up in the roughest part of Manchester, and how if someone had told him as little as four years ago that he would be spearheading England's World Cup bid, he would never have believed them. He said that football changed his life, as it has changed the lives of millions of people all over the world.

Prime Minister David Cameron said that with our passion for the game, we could have created the most spectacular World Cup in history, but that now we have to accept that Russia and Qatar have the 2018 and 2022 World Cups, and it's time now to embrace them.

This is the first time ever these countries will host the competition and have this wonderful opportunity where the eyes of the world will be upon them. The World Cup Final is the most watched event in the whole world: a staggering billion people will tune in. Remarkable when you consider that so many people in this world don't have access to clean water, let alone a television.

Both the Russian contingent and the Qatar contingent said they won't let us down. I truly hope not, as Russia is known for having racism problems in many parts of the country. Premier Footballer Peter Odemwingie, from West Bromwich Albion, said he believes the amount of discrimination in the country is on the rise and is a real concern for the 2018 World Cup. Odemwingie received racial abuse from Lokomotiv fans when he was a player on the Russian side; his own fans targeted him for abuse. How will they treat fans from other countries, such as the African nations, is now the question?

The Russian people, who are against racism, in general the majority of the nation, hope this World Cup goes a long way to kicking racism out of the game for good in Russia. Everyone should be welcomed with no prejudice against any colour or nationality.

It is a shame we didn't get the World Cup. We have waited forty-four years since the last one and it would have meant so much to the economy, the people and the country. After the doom and gloom of the credit crunch and times of hardship in Britain, this would have been something wonderful to look forward to.

Many of us may not be around the next time Britain hosts the World Cup, but our children and grandchildren will, that's for sure. We are too great a nation, too passionate about the game to be overlooked again for long.

For now, we can look forward to the Olympics and the eyes of the world will be on us for that. Let's show them the pride and ability of this nation to put on a show like no other. And, always remember, we had the World Cup just once, and we won it, that can never be taken away from us.

## *JJ*

## Brixton

When I left the small South Wales valleys to make a new life in London, my first home was in Brixton. I couldn't believe how multicultural it was at that time. It was all new to me, living, enjoying and venturing into another culture.

I can remember thinking 'I'm in heaven', mixing with an array of people from all different backgrounds from all over the world. My Jamaican boyfriend at the time started to teach me how to cook Caribbean food. He took me to Brixton market and my eyes opened wide with excitement when I saw all the stalls full to the brim with exotic foods, the likes of which I had never seen nor heard of before. It was a huge rush to the senses, all those magnificent colours, tastes and smells bombarding me everywhere I turned. Coming from a fruit merchant family, I had seen beautifully coloured fruits before, but nothing like this.

I remember we bought ox tail and even cow foot. Like everyone back home, the only ox tail I had eaten was in the mass produced tins of soup we all know and love. I simply couldn't wait to get home and start cooking.

We walked past stalls blasting out all the latest Reggae and Ska music that came directly from Jamaica. To hear this unknown music in a setting as surreal to me as a market was an amazing experience, and the atmosphere was breath-taking.

At the time, Brixton had a bad and notorious reputation. Whenever it came up in conversation, the reaction would always be along the lines of "Oh you're not going there, are you?" and when I replied that

I lived there, the look on their faces would be a picture. To me, it was wonderful, it was home. Granted you have to be careful wherever you are in this world and staying safe is paramount, but I didn't see Brixton through the eyes of people who had never been there, I viewed it through my eyes as my home.

At night we would go to a shabean called Cons which was situated down in a basement. The place was always full to the rafters with people drinking the famous Jamaican rum, Appleton, and champagne whilst listening to the latest Reggae music.

I remember Bob Marley featured heavily on the play list at the time. I actually went to see him play live at Crystal Palace; he was truly outstanding, an icon. There were thousands of people from all over the UK there, it was like looking at a sea of people, bobbing their heads up and down to the music, and every nationality was represented, such an eclectic mix.

There was a restaurant in Brixton called Chin's. The owner, Chin, was a Chinese-Jamaican mix and the food was out of this world. Then just a few streets away in Villa Road was a blues dance which had the quickly growing reputation for being the best blues venue in London. A 'blues' was the term given to an illegal house party where anyone and everyone was welcome. The Jamaicans would bring their sound systems with them from back home to fill the venue with intense beats and encapsulating music.

I guess the reason blues were so popular is that the Jamaicans would have had enough of the prejudice against them and the hassle of being constantly turned away from the mainstream clubs and decided to hold their own parties. I and many others were grateful they did, as it was such an exhilarating experience. I was entering into a new, exciting world and I couldn't get enough of it.

It wasn't only Brixton where you could find blues dance, it was wherever there was a Jamaican community within the UK. These communities were nicknamed 'Ghettos'. They literally turned their homes at weekends into their very own nightclubs, moving the furniture out and just having a sound system and a makeshift bar. I remember the white males, known as skinheads, would also join in, in a completely friendly way. They also loved the Reggae and Ska music and many of them had Jamaican girlfriends. It was great to see two very different types of people joining together in a recreational way every weekend.

The skinheads would also dress like their Jamaican friends, donning the pork pie hats, crombi jackets and stay press jeans. I believe the whole ensemble of the skinheads in those days was inspired by the Jamaican boys. This is why I don't understand the stigma of skinheads being racist, as all I saw when they were together was unity and friendship. It was a pleasure to witness it first-hand.

Then came the awful Brixton riots of 1981. This, in turn, engulfed Jamaican communities all over Britain. The Sus Law was to blame, a law that gave police the power to stop and search anyone at any time. They seemed to target innocent black and mixed race men much more than any others, an act which brought widespread condemnation and hatred in return. A lot of the time things escalated, something I experienced myself with my former boyfriend at the time.

The riots sent shockwaves throughout Britain. The night it all started in Brixton all I could hear were sirens and shouting in the streets. There was an intense and terrifying smell of burning in the air, a smell that made me think the whole of Brixton was on fire. It really was horrifying and extremely scary.

Scenes like that should never be repeated in this country. The Sus Law was itself deemed to be highly suspect and in turn was abolished soon after.

Brixton has come a long way since the 1970s and 80s. Like Britain as a whole, it is far more multicultural these days. I am intrigued to learn that Brixton even has its own currency now, 'the Brixton pound', and its aim is to keep the currency within the community to help small businesses thrive. I think this is an excellent idea and I wish it every success. It is this kind of spirit and togetherness which makes the area stand out, people united, together for each other.

Indeed, it is these people that made Brixton every inch it is today and it has become an area that many people want to live in. People from all origins mixing and habiting in harmony. Everyone has a reason why they want to explore the area more. Mine was my love of Reggae music that drove me to want to mix and live with the people and see their side of life.

I know that Reggae music has given me a sense of history that I would never have embraced without it. I have had the life-changing opportunity to mix and see so much diversity and culture, an opportunity unheard of for so many people back home in South Wales. This has all combined to make up my fibres of life and made me into the person I am today. It has been a journey, the journey of my life, which will keep on going as I still try to explore more and more about the lives of others, and what better place to have started this journey than in Brixton.

I am proud of my life, and proud that I lived in, and I loved, Brixton.

*JJ*